MW00716920

HIGH IMPACT CHURCH PLANTING
You can lead a Harvest Directed Ministry

"If you want to start a church that will make a difference in your community, this is the book to read!" **Tom Mercer**, *Senior Pastor, High Desert Church (www.highdesertchurch.com)*

Dr. John Jackson
Senior Pastor, Carson Valley Christian Center
www.carsonvalleychristiancenter.com
© VisionQuest Ministries, 2000

ISBN 0-9716489-1-3 $15.95

Unless otherwise indicated, all Scripture quotations are from HOLY BIBLE, The New International Version of the Bible (NIV) © 1973, 1978, 1984 by the International Bible Society. Used by permission of Zondervan Bible Publishers.

TABLE OF CONTENTS

Foreword & Acknowledgments............................3
Chapter 1: Dare to Dream Big Dreams for God.........4
Chapter 2: You Left a Secure Job to Do What?............12
Chapter 3: One Example of High Impact Ministry.....19
Chapter 4: The DNA of High Impact Churches.........28
Chapter 5: A New Paradigm for Church Planting......38
Chapter 6: Starting a New Work: 11 Strategic Steps..48
Chapter 7: Up Close and Personal........................57
Epilogue:...64
Appendix of Resources.....................................65

Foreword & Acknowledgements

God loves adventure! You can hardly read the pages of Scripture without seeing the hand of God at work, taking people to places they never thought possible (think Moses, Abraham, Daniel, Ruth, Paul, among others).

High Impact Church Planting has been that kind of journey for me and for our family. What we first thought ridiculous (the idea that we could start a large church that would impact our world in huge ways) has now become reality. What an amazing journey!

I want to acknowledge the wonderful models of ministry in a number of gifted colleagues and mentors who have impacted me up close or from a distance over the years include: Conrad Lowe, Glenn Gunderson, Tom Mercer, Jack Hamilton, Dane Aaker, Graydon Jessup, George Barna, John Maxwell, Bill Easum, Rick Warren, Bill Hybels, Carl George, Paul Borden, Jack Hayford, and a host of others have been "giants" in ministry for me. Any worthy insights in this book may have originated with them; any mistakes are mine alone.

I want to thank my parents, Marvin & Millie Jackson, for their steadfast love of Jesus, even in the midst of sometimes difficult seasons. Dad went to be with Jesus this year in a tragic accident…but I know he loved the story of changed lives that our High Impact Church is living out! My brothers and sister and their families are a constant source of encouragement and strength. My wife's family is a joyous blessing to our lives. Our staff and church family at Carson Valley Christian Center have made this adventure worth living! Steve and Kirsten Wilson have helped in the editing of this manuscript and for that, I'm grateful (and you will be too!).

In closing, my children Jennifer, Dena, Rachel, Joshua, and Harrison are the joys of my life. They made writing this a joy. My wife Pamela is a model mother and a treasured wife to me. To her, in the name of Jesus, I dedicate this book. It is my prayer that God will enrich your heart and expand your vision with this resource.

Chapter 1
Dare to Dream Big Dreams for God

I first heard God speak the phrase, "Will you dare to dream big dreams for Me?" at a snow-covered church campground in March of 1996. My first response was "No!" I had been wrestling with God for quite some time about my future in ministry. And now, shortly after reading the story of a well known church planter (Rick Warren, <u>Purpose Driven Church</u>), God seemed to be speaking into my heart as well. A dream of a local church that would reach unchurched people and change the world started to form in my heart. My initial icy response to God melted as the fire of passion began to burn in my heart.

Many of us are initially reluctant to dream big. Intuitively, we know that dreaming big most often leads to big change in our lives and ministries. And big change means risk, means stepping out of comfort zones, means climbing out of ruts. Yet I am convinced that God may well be asking many of you the same question he asked me in 1998: "Will you dare to dream big dreams for me?" I am praying that God will melt whatever icy responses may lurk in your hearts and light His passionate dream for ministry in your heart.

Please do me two favors before you continue further into this chapter: First, can you dream a really big dream of what God could do if there were no obstacles in the way? *Five years from now, if there were no limitations on finances, leadership, facilities, or programs, what could God do in you and through you to make an impact on your world through your local church?* Can you see that picture clearly? What would worship look like? How would fellowship, discipleship, evangelism, and ministry be taking place? What life changes would people be experiencing in the context of your dream? Make sure that you see every ministry dimension with some measure of clarity.

Carson Valley Christian Center
Our 5 Year Dream

- Reach 1,000 adults in weekend worship within five years of our first public worship service

- Have a minimum of 20 acres of property, with worship center seating capacity of 1,000

- 40 % of those attending worship be previously unchurched

- 50 % of those attending weekend worship using spiritual gifts for ministry, involved in a small group, and have completed personal discipleship training

- Plant one new church per year after five years

Once you have that picture clearly in mind, do me a second favor.

Take every dimension of your 5-year dream and get it clearly in view. *Now, multiply every dimension by a factor of 10 and let your spirit, heart, and mind soar as you consider what God could do that would be 10 times your largest dream.* If you are able to envision that, you just might be grasping what God is able to do if you raise your leadership lid and cooperate with Him in His agenda for our lives.

Thinking about a local church that powerfully prevails against the presence of hell in its community is energizing. But most pastoral leaders have felt the opposite in our churches. We've watched, participated in, or led churches that could use a strong dose of hope (or electric shock treatment!). Worse yet, we are clear that God is calling us to lead those same churches to health and vitality! *What if we could plant seed in such a way that the soil would bear 30-60-100 fold returns?* Those are the dreams of church leaders who want to reach their community through High Impact Churches.

Definition: High Impact Churches break through spiritual, social, and leadership barriers to establish new churches, new ministries, and reach large numbers of new people for Christ. High Impact churches confront the law of inertia and the reality of human lethargy with a passionate purposeful pursuit of God's plan for evangelism in their area.

Dreaming is fine, but reality must be faced. The truth is, there is no county in America has a higher percentage of churched persons today than a decade ago (According to the American Society for Church Growth).

In addition:

* The estimated US unchurched population is over 195 million (Gallup)
* In 1995, it was reported that the previous 10 years Protestant population had declined by 9.5% while the general US population has increased by 11.4%
* The church to population ratio is declining (1900-27 churches per 10,000, 1950-17, and 1996-11)
* The U.S. loses 72.11 churches each week, and gains 24.03 per week (net loss of 58 churches per week)
* The U.S. is the largest post-Christian nation on earth and the 3rd largest unchurched nation.
* The U.S. leads the world in every category of violent and domestic crime and social decay

Given these rather sobering statistics, some have said that the church is "dangerously close to 'dancing with dinosaurs' before tar pits of doom". William Easum has written about 7 assumptions that the church would do well to hold as we move into the 21st century:

1) North America is the new mission field
2) Society will become increasingly hostile toward Christianity in the twenty-first century
3) The distinction between clergy and laity will disappear in the twenty-first century
4) If churches only improve what they have been doing, they will die
5) The best way to fail today is to improve yesterday's successes
6) Bureaucracies and traditional practices are the major cause of the decline of most denominations in North America
7) Traditional churches that thrive in the twenty-first century will initiate radical change before the year 2001. (William Easum, Dancing with Dinosaurs, p. 13-14, www.easumbandy.com)

George Barna goes one step further when he says, "Let's cut to the chase. After nearly two decades of studying Christian churches in America, I'm convinced that the typical church as we know it today has a rapidly expiring shelf life" (Barna, The Second Coming of the Church, p. 1)

So, why would anyone consider investing his or her life in the ministry of the local church? Only two words make the proposition worth considering: Great Commission. Jesus Christ not only gave us the assignment of reaching and teaching people, He also gave us the vehicle with which to travel that road. The local church is where one can know Christ, grow in Him, and experience all of God's family business. Having an impact for Christ in your world is what this book is all about.

"Then Jesus came to them and said, "All authority in heaven and on earth has been given to me. Therefore go and make disciples of all nations, baptizing them in the name of the Father and of the Son and of the Holy Spirit, and teaching them to obey everything I have commanded you. And surely I am with you always, to the very end of the age." (The Great Commission, Matthew 28:18-20).

The Great Commission is the defining purpose of the church of Jesus Christ. Evangelism is the only thing that we are called to do here that we will not be able to do in eternity. For us to fulfill God's game plan for ministry we simply have to make the Great Commission front and center of all we do. High Impact Church Ministry keeps the Great Commission as its focus. A passion for reaching people who are not in relationship with Christ is *"job 1"* for those whom God calls to start and lead High Impact Churches. I invite you to "Dare to Dream" with me of what starting or leading a High Impact Church could mean for your ministry and for fulfilling the Great Commission.

KEY TRANSFERABLE CONCEPT:

All High Impact Churches start with a big dream. You will never plant a High Impact Church until God has firmly placed His dream within your heart Here's a well known example of a God-sized dream that launched a High Impact Church:

The Saddleback Vision
From Pastor Rick's first sermon, March 30, 1980

It is the dream of a place where the hurting, the depressed, the frustrated, and the confused can find love, acceptance, help, hope, forgiveness, guidance, and encouragement.

It is the dream of sharing the Good News of Jesus Christ with the hundreds of thousands of residents in south Orange County.

It is the dream of welcoming 20,000 members into the fellowship of our church family—loving, learning, laughing, and living in harmony together.

It is the dream of developing people to spiritual maturity through Bible studies, small groups, seminars, retreats, and a Bible school for our members.

It is the dream of equipping every believer for a significant ministry by helping them discover the gifts and talents God gave them.

It is the dream of sending out hundreds of career missionaries and church workers all around the world, and empowering every member for a personal life mission in the world. It is the dream of sending our members by the thousands on short-term mission projects to every continent. It is the dream of starting at least one new daughter church every year.

It is the dream of at least fifty acres of land, on which will be built a regional church for south Orange County—with beautiful, yet simple, facilities including a worship center seating thousands, a counseling and prayer center, classrooms for Bible studies and training lay ministers, and a recreation area. All of this will be designed to minister to the total person—spiritually, emotionally, physically, and socially—and set in a peaceful, inspiring garden landscape.

I stand before you today and state in confident assurance that these dreams will become reality. Why? Because they are inspired by God! (*The Purpose Driven Church*, Rick Warren, p. 43, Copyright Zondervan Publishing, Inc., Used by permission of Zondervan)

SELF STUDY ACTIVITIES:

Activity One: Dream Break

If you didn't answer these questions fully as you began this chapter, give yourself a block of time to do so now: Five years from now, if there were no limitations on finances, leadership, facilities, or programs, what could God do in you and through you to make an impact on your world through your local church? Paint that picture clearly in your mind, and then write it down on paper.

Now, take every dimension of your 5-year dream and multiply it by a factor of ten. Let your spirit, heart, and mind soar as you consider what God could do that would be 10 times your largest dream. If you are able to envision that, you just might be beginning to grasp what God is able to do if you raise your leadership lid and cooperate with Him in His agenda for your life.

Activity Two: Research your Community

National statistics can be compelling; local statistics are more so. See how many of these questions you can answer for your particular community:

What is the unchurched population in your community?

By what percentage has the Protestant population in your community increased or decreased over the past 10 years? How does that compare to the increase or decrease in the general population?

What is the church-to-population ratio in your community? What was it in 1950?

How many churches has your community gained in the last 3 years? How many churches has it lost?

Activity Three: Bible Study and Application

Read Matthew 28:18-20.

If your church has a vision or purpose statement, how does it incorporate the ideas of the Great Commission?

The Great Commission commands us to make disciples of all nations by going, baptizing and teaching people to obey all that Jesus commanded. How would you evaluate your church (strengths and weaknesses) in each of those areas?

Chapter 2
You Left a Secure Job to Do What?

Yes, we left a secure denominational job with wonderful friends and great supportive people in our lives to plant a church to reach unchurched people. We planted Carson Valley Christian Center (CVC) in another state, apart from where we had been raised, in a place where we literally knew nobody. Ours was a pioneering church plant, the toughest kind and the most dubious of success. Were we sure this was God's leading? Absolutely! But the story begins long before that decision.

I was born and raised in a pastor's home. Dad and Mom served several small to medium sized churches (150-400 people); we experienced the highs and lows of local church ministry during the 60's and 70's. I not only was fortunate to have loving parents, but regardless of the church experience, my parents kept our focus on the Lord, and not the church.

Despite years of being told that I should be a "pastor, just like your dad", I was determined to pursue a vocation other than the church. In fact, I literally told God that I would do anything at all to serve Him except for two things: I would NOT be a missionary or minister. That changed in an evening service at the age of 16 with my Dad preaching. During that service, I sensed God's specific call to vocational ministry. Later that year I was to meet the woman that God had specifically prepared for me as a life partner. At age 18, Pamela and I were married and we began the great adventure of following God in ministry.

The next several years included completing college and seminary, all the while serving part and full-time in the church (often it was full-time work and part time pay!). In 1987, after serving 7 years in staff roles at a medium sized church in Southern California, I became the Senior Pastor at the age of 26. Over the next five years, God worked in wonderful ways to bring healing and growth and we "settled in" for the long haul. But God had other plans.

Our denominational family was struggling. Though I had previously served as the elected President of the denominational agency, I never considered myself a denominational leader. After a leadership transition, I was asked to consider allowing my name to be submitted for the CEO role. I flatly said "NO!" I lived 1 mile from the beach in a semi-rural area and was leading a church full of wonderful people who loved me and cared for my family. The denominational agency was located 25 miles east of Los Angeles in a smog-filled, asphalt-covered population center. Financial troubles had plagued the mission agency; baptisms had substantially declined and many churches were caught in a death spiral.

After a long and tortuous process of prayer and preparation, God clearly moved us to become the Executive Minister and CEO of our denominational agency. At the age of 31, I became the youngest denominational executive in the history of our denomination. In this role, I was able to give leadership to 280 churches with over 50,000 members in 4 states. Four and one half years of ministry were full of exciting developments. Financial health was restored with a new controller at the helm; missions giving and baptisms increased substantially over this period. External indicators all looked positive. But, I was restless to get back to the ministry of the local church. Our "home church" was an exciting place that made me hunger to "get back in the saddle" of local church ministry.

While considering several ministry options, I simply could not get a sense of God's direction. I kept having a stirring about planting a local church. During that time, I was able to read an advance copy of Rick Warren's award winning book, "Purpose Driven Church". About 40 pages into the book, I read Warren's vision announced at the first public meeting of the church in 1980. When I read it, I laughed—out loud! Who would have the audacity to announce such a thing on their first public meeting date? Then, it was as though God Himself spoke to me. "John, would you be willing to dare to dream big dreams for Me?" I was stunned. But, I regained my composure enough to say, "No!"

As a young denominational executive, I had a secure position, good salary, and bright prospects for the future. Yes, I was unsettled outside the local church. But, plant a church? All the church plants I had participated in had been fairly small. Many of them had failed in the first three years. My gift mix (leadership, teaching, and administration) seemed most suited for serving large ministries. How could God be moving me in this direction? It was here that my wife Pam and my brother and sister-in-law (Gene and Barbara) began to be part of the vision confirmation process.

A searching walk in the woods in a campground in Wisconsin (in March!) culminated months of agonizing and finally led to a sense of freedom. Yes, God was in this! We could move forward with prayerful consideration of how God might be leading us. We were specifically led to consider an area we had visited on vacation many times. The Carson Valley/Carson City area in Northern Nevada was geographically beautiful and spiritually desolate. Research indicated that fewer than 5% of the people in the area attended church on a given week. Now we had a specific geography, and a specific ministry focus to pray about. Gene and Barbara agreed to join us in the adventure and sell their business and home to join on the journey. By fall of 1996, after prayer with family members, we were ready to move further out on the edge of faith.

We were definitely living on the edge of faith!

On October 16, 1996, I announced my resignation to our board leaders. I had a vision and a dream for a church. I had no financial commitments for support, no idea what would lie ahead for our family and lots of apprehension. But the vision was burning a hole in our heart and we simply had to move where we believed God was taking us.

Immediately, God began to open huge doors of opportunity. I was asked to stay for five months in my leadership role (an unheard of time frame for a denominational resignation). I committed to strong leadership during that time, and was afforded the opportunity to develop a specific funding plan for the church. I knew I would have to get a job or start a business until we could get the church up to a point of strength where I could be supported full time.

Doors of opportunity were not the only thing that opened during this time. Two other major factors became clear to us that became part of the process of launching a High Impact Church. The first was the issue of fundraising. Most pastors are hesitant to speak about money and most church planters want someone else to raise the money while they do the ministry. But, *a High Impact Church leader must have the ability to cast a compelling vision and be the lead fundraiser for the ministry.* We were to learn some powerful lessons in this regard as God worked through our vision casting with various people and agencies.

God's hand was with us so much so that $250,000 was committed by 3 different entities. A denominational agency gave $100,000 over 2 ½ years. A local church also committed $100,000 over 3 years. Interestingly, my brother Gene and his wife Barbara had served as Elders in this church, but I had no specific involvement here. This is a visionary church with a passionate commitment to the Great Commission! We also wrote that familiar but dreaded, "missionary letter" to our Christmas card list. Over $50,000 was committed by dear and wonderful people and churches that had known, loved, and prayed for us over the course of years. We were awed and humbled! It became clear immediately that I should work full-time to launch this church as a High Impact Ministry.

Our second major vision casting exercise was to develop a team of leaders. In our case we met with and personally challenged about five families to go with us to the Carson Valley. Roy and Tracy Conover became part of the original launch team and their good friends Jack & Cheri-Li Negrete already lived in Carson Valley and became part of the team as well. Carson Valley Christian Center was launched with 8 adults, 12 children, and a boatload of vision and faith. Now, some four years later, every one of the original core families remains with us and remains committed to the vision that God gave us at the start.

KEY TRANSFERABLE CONCEPTS:

High Impact Church Leaders are impelled to action by God's Big Dream. You can't be lethargic about God's calling. The vision has to grab you.

High Impact Church Leaders must be able to raise significant monies for God's vision. We believe that $100-200k is probably a minimum start-up number in most settings.

High Impact Church Leaders are able to cast vision so that key leaders rally and become part of the team

High Impact Church leaders are catalysts. They are able to lead a team of leaders.

SELF STUDY ACTIVITIES:

Activity One: Bible Study and Application:
                 God's Audacious Plans

Read Genesis 17:15-17; 18:1-15; 21:1-7
What are some of the reasons that Abraham and Sarah laughed at God's plans?
Who had the last laugh? Why?
When have you laughed at one of God's plans? How did the situation turn out?

Activity Two: Reflection

Look back over your ministry journey. How would you chart the journey God's taken you on? Looking over your chart, what is your current ministry trajectory?

Have you sensed any "stirrings" from God that might alter or adjust your trajectory? How open are you to those stirrings?

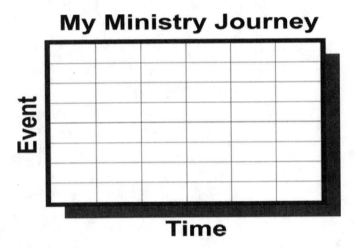

Activity Three: Book Study

Read or review Rick Warren's book, *The Purpose Driven Church*. Meet with a colleague who has also read the book and discuss Warren's points. Do you agree or disagree? What is God calling you to do in ministry based on what you've learned?

Activity Four: Personal Evaluation

Do you believe in God's dream in your life enough to risk raising money from friends and family for the dream?

Read II Corinthians 2:12-13. Paul describes having no peace in Troas because Titus was not there with him. Who would you love to do ministry with? Can you envision casting a vision for ministry that would hit their heart? Are you a team builder or a lone ranger in ministry?

Chapter 3
One Example of High Impact Ministry: The CVC Story

Have you ever noticed that one of the best ways to get a group of mothers involved in animated discussion is to get them telling the stories of their children's births? All it takes is a newly pregnant woman in their midst, and suddenly, epic stories of 36-hour labors and fervent testimonies to the beauty of an epidural fly through the room. Accounts of pregnancy and delivery spill over one another as the mothers happily initiate the newcomer into the club of motherhood. And unless the new mother-to-be's eyes glaze over at the sheer volume of experiences offered her, she will eagerly listen and glean what she can from each story, tucking "take away ideas" into her mental motherhood file. Intuitively, she knows that as much as she'll learn from books and from her doctor, there is a special power in story that cannot be ignored.

There may be a high-impact ministry inside of you that will be birthed sometime in the near future. My advice would be to use your "expectant" time to the fullest, reading books, consulting experts…and listening to birth stories. Those who have had a part in birthing a high impact church or ministry usually don't need much prompting to tell their story. I know I don't. And if we were sitting down over a cup of coffee, and you asked for my story, here's part of what I'd say about the birth of CVC:

Our commitment from the beginning was to establish a church that would quickly break through growth and community penetration barriers. To do this, I knew we would need a team of people. I had experienced many churches "imploding" in their early life with a lack of leadership sufficient for the ministry needs. God answered this prayer in a specific and tangible way.

Gene & Barbara (my brother and sister-in-law) had been "on-board" from the beginning. They brought huge commitment, stability, and tremendous gifts for ministry. Roy & Tracy received our vision letter and told us they had been praying for a specific mission assignment. Both of them had participated in our youth ministry in Southern California, had served in short term mission trips, and had been part of a church plant (with some pain!) from that same church. Not only were they called to join us and sell their homes and quit their jobs, but it turned out they knew someone living in Carson Valley!!! Jacque and Cheri joined us as soon as we moved here (they were long time friends of Roy & Tracy's). The first leadership team of CVC was born: 8 adults and 12 children became the birthing coaches for the ministry.

Many stories of that early time revolve around the sacrifices of people from our "Christmas Card" list. Gordon and Freeda (a couple in their 90's living in Florida) stayed with my family when we were all young children. While they had no children of their own, they stayed with us while our parents were on an extended trip. Gordon and Freeda lived on fixed incomes, but they gave $50 per month each month to a work they would never see to reach people they would never know on this side of heaven.

Steve and Kim (a couple in their 30's living in Spain with the Navy Seabees), gave $25 per month after receiving our letter. Over 50 other people gave in amounts ranging from $10 to $200 each month. Every time a letter came in the mail it was a reminder of God's grace work in His people. It was also a sobering reminder of our accountability for God's work at Carson Valley Christian Center.

Shortly after arriving in Carson Valley in April of 1997, we began to plant the church. I think. Boy was I confused. I left a busy office and a busy schedule and moved to a new area with no relationships and no office. I remember sitting in the guesthouse on our property that was used as "command central" for the church. I had a game plan on paper. I had lots of dreams. But, I had no people! How was a "High Impact Church" to be established with no people? I remember the day I spent an hour with my neighbor (an unbeliever) and then left his home saying "I've got to get to work". God stopped me cold in my tracks. He said,

"What do you think you have been doing?" Some church planter I was turning out to be.

After a month of getting settled, the three families who had moved to Carson Valley (the fourth family moved two months later) began meeting in a home group and developing relationships. Relationship building often meant going to the country store down the street (the owners of which now attend our church), hanging around the post office or local McDonalds, and talking with repair people who would come to our house during the move-in process.

We spent lots of time in prayer and sharing those first few months. Faith Promise Partners living outside Carson Valley had committed over 2000 hours of prayer per month; those in the core team also committed many hours of prayer within the early months of the church. We determined to hold a BBQ at our home in July and invited every person we knew. That totaled about 50 people including out of town relatives!

Other than Bible Study, we committed to worship together at local churches. It had been my hope to not start a Sunday gathering until about 3-4 months before our February, 1998 launch. It turned out that most local churches were uncomfortable with us attending; so on the last Sunday of July in 1997, we met at a Lazer Tag amusement facility with about 25 people.

We started to meet each Sunday on one condition: *no non-Christians would be invited to these gatherings*. These were "core group" meetings, not outreach events.

During this same time frame, God opened a miraculous door and we were able to purchase 39 acres of property in our target geographical area at a price of $270,000 (a $170,000 reduction from the market value!). Because the church had no money, two core families secured the land personally with assets the Lord had provided.

Another BBQ was held in August at Gene and Barbara's home and 85 people attended! This was exciting. Though we had about 35 people now participating regularly, many of our people had never been in a larger church and I knew they really needed to see an example to grasp the concept. So, in September, we visited Bayside Church in Sacramento with 23 of our people. The Senior Pastor, Ray Johnston, gave us 30 valuable minutes in a local pizza parlor and answered questions. He gave us a high-impact "take-away" idea: do preview services as a way to reach potential core group members and do pre-evangelism in the community. In the two-hour ride back home, we decided to do our first preview 3 weeks later!

Our first Preview Service in September of 1997 started an awesome pattern. We had 145 people in attendance and 12 people prayed to receive Christ. Our first Discovery 101 class was held that day and 47 people attended! For 3 weeks, we met in a casino/hotel in Minden, and then moved to a Carson City casino where we stayed for 5 months. We had preview services in October (175 people) and November (202 people). Each time we had 20+ people join what we started calling our "launch team" and we had people pray to receive Christ! Discovery 101 classes were held each preview service afternoon, and we followed up with Discovery 201 and 301 classes as well. All services and classes were held in a section of the casino ballroom; we were committed to being non-traditional from the start.

MEMORY SNAPSHOT

Along the way to our public launch of the church, we did some crazy things. Here's a snapshot of just one wild moment in the birth of CVC.

For five months, our fledgling church met in a Carson City casino's banquet rooms. On a Saturday evening in December 1997, two of us loaded a jacuzzi onto a rental truck, drove it to the casino, and physically carried it up to the second floor through a hallway crowded with catering staff. We filled the jacuzzi with hot water through 100 feet of garden hose hooked up to a water heater.

And then the next morning, with 20 degree weather outside, steam rising from the heated water and a cold wind whistling through the inside, we baptized thirteen people in the jacuzzi in a second-floor back hallway of a Nevada casino. Those 13 will never forget that day of their spiritual journey.

It doesn't get any better than that.

By January of 1998 we were able to locate a warehouse facility and Douglas County affirmed our leasing of the facility on one condition: we had to pull a building permit at a cost of $100,000 and promise to complete our new facility on our land in 12 months. We pursued every alternative avenue, but it seemed clear that this was to be our pathway (as an aside, I DO NOT recommend building or buying anything in the first 3-5 years of a normal church start—it just happened to be God's provision and plan for CVC). In less than 30 days, we built out 10,000 square feet of the empty warehouse and were able to worship in the building one week before launch Sunday. The Sunday before our public launch we had 100 adults and 45 children in attendance.

In the 8 weeks prior to our launch, we really pushed our people and community towards the launch date of February 22nd. You can only "go public" once. So we went with all our heart and soul. We did creative direct mail, newspaper inserts, posters, personal handout cards, and a variety of other outreach mechanisms to homes and businesses. We told all of our people that they were at a terminal in Cape Canaveral. "We're launching a church instead of a rocket—and what you do in your role can make the difference in the entire project". On Launch Sunday, we had 100 adults in our team, and 65 of them had a specific service role in the life of the church.

On Launch Sunday, 424 people attended and there were more than 20 decisions for Christ. We were ecstatic! The next 18 months were a journey of God's continuous stretching of our faith and vision. We had 674 people the first Easter, added two services in June of 1998, had over 1300 people in Easter of 1999, raised just over $300,000 towards the new building in 1998 & 1999, and moved to our 39 acre property in an 18,000 square foot multi-purpose building in October of 1999. The total land, buildings and equipment cost at this stage exceeded $2.5 million dollars. We borrowed heavily from friends in ministry and were awed at how God kept meeting needs. Our key leaders sacrificed greatly to see these steps take place.

CVC was reaching 750 people in worship at the end of 1999, and by our second birthday in 2000 we were over 850 people each week. Over 2450 people attended Easter 2000 and by May of 2000 CVC was averaging just under 900 people in attendance. As I write this today in the fall of 2001, over 1200 people are involved each weekend at CVC and over 400 are connected in a midweek activity (ministry or group). 40% of those attending CVC today were unchurched prior to attending CVC (meaning no church involvement in the six months prior to CVC).

Expectant times are full of nervousness, stress, and a need for clear thinking! You may be in a significant "expectant" time of ministry now, or you might see one in your near future. Either way, my challenge to you is to seize the moment and learn as much as you can. When it happens, take a lot of pictures, record your memories, and share them with others who hope one day to birth their own exciting ministry.

KEY TRANSFERABLE CONCEPTS:

Birthing a High Impact Church takes time. Casting a vision to key leaders who will become your team is critical. Developing vision that moves people into risking today for the promise of tomorrow is essential.

High Impact Churches are built with people who are willing to sacrifice. Insure that key leaders you recruit are healthy in their relationships and are able to sacrifice for the vision. The stability of marriages and family in your leadership team should be rock solid.

High Impact Leadership teams should have broad focus and varied expertise. The Senior Pastoral leader must be secure enough to lead the leaders without fear of the gifts within the team

SELF STUDY ACTIVITIES:

Activity One:

Make note of any "take away ideas" for your ministry that come out of CVC's birth story.

Find a new church in a nearby community. Meet with a member of the church's staff or core leadership team and hear about the "birth" of the church. Make a note of any "take away" ideas that come out of your listening to their birth story. Compare and contrast what you observe in their story with what you have read of the CVC story. Which parts of either story stir your heartbeat for ministry? How will those "heartbeats" be present in your High Impact Church Plant?

Activity Two:

Make a list of unchurched people you're in contact with during the course of a week. Referring back to your list, ask yourself the following questions:

Do you rush through your interactions with these people or watch for the opportunities God may give you to nudge them closer to him?

Remember my story…I thought work was the organization and infrastructure, not the interactions with people. Hopefully you'll be further down the road than I was!

Do you consider your interactions with unchurched people part of your vocation? Why or why not? We built our relationships at the stores, post office, community events, etc. Is that ministry? Does it "count" for your sense of what ministry is?

Consider: How is your leadership team at building relationships with unchurched people? What could you do as a team to nurture a climate that values meaningful interactions with the unchurched people in your community?

Activity Three: Bible Study

Read Hebrews 11:1-12:1
Why does the author of Hebrews tell the stories of so many men and women of faith? What did he hope to accomplish in the lives of his readers? How does hearing the stories of others obedient to God's call help us in fulfilling God's call on our own lives (see 12:1)?

Make note of any "take away" ideas from this passage for your own life and ministry.

Chapter 4
The DNA of High Impact Churches

On July 4, 1999 over 2700 people came to 2221 Meridian Blvd. to receive a free gift from Carson Valley Christian Center (CVC). Just over 16 months old, the church was already impacting hundreds of lives each week. And now, with this Big Event (one of CVC's core strategies), thousands of people were being touched. On that day, several people approached CVC leaders and tried to press money into our hands. Others came with tears in their eyes to say "thank you" for giving their children the opportunity to enjoy rides, games and food...all for FREE. The truth is the price had already been paid...

God is clearly the one who brings to life a ministry like CVC. As I write now, we are not quite 4 years old and are seeing over 1,200 people attending worship each weekend. Over 40% of CVC attendees were either "de-churched" (no church attendance 6 months prior to CVC, but did have a church background), or "un-churched". Is this just an isolated miracle of God at CVC or is it possible to identify principles for starting and leading a High Impact Church?

I contend that there are principles in play here. God wants churches that make an impact in their local communities. He may be calling you to start or lead such a church; if so, what are the essential characteristics of a High Impact Church?

Let's review the definition of a High Impact Church:

High Impact Churches break through spiritual, social, and leadership barriers to establish new churches, new ministries, and reach new people for Christ. High Impact churches confront the law of inertia and the reality of human lethargy with a passionate purposeful pursuit of God's plan for evangelism in their area.

Lyle Schaller has written a book entitled, "The Very Large Church". In that work he explains that social environments have become much more complex, anonymous and hostile. Larger institutions are in the fabric of our society and therefore larger churches are an increasingly large part of our world. Since "large" is such a part of the social landscape, Schaller suggests that we need large churches to significantly impact those born after 1965.

Schaller then boldly proclaims that effort should be put into planting large churches designed to reach 700 people after 7 years. *High Impact Church Planting meets this need in our day.* Existing churches have to find ways to break through these barriers as well and can use the principles below to chart their course.

At this juncture, many will object that High Impact Churches are only concerned with size. I would challenge those wrestling with this to consider the Great Commission in Matthew 28:18-20 and the Acts 1:8 charge as mandates for reaching all the lost that can be reached. In Matthew 22:1-14, Jesus' parable about the king's invitation to the wedding banquet is analogous to my view of why churches should not rest until they have reached into every corner of their world.

High Impact Church Planting takes an aggressive stance; particularly in contrast to the typical approach to church planting. Most new church plants start with several strikes against them, most notably that they start small and remain small. Barna observed this phenomenon when he commented, "Unfortunately, most of the churches begun have been doomed from the get-go. Typically they launch with the wrong individual in charge (pastors who are not the catalytic, entrepreneurial leaders required), with an inadequate core group (based on the number and nature of the people involved), an outdated model, and severe undercapitalization." (Barna, The Second Coming of the Church, p. 27)

High Impact Churches not only share specific outcomes orientation, they also manifest some common leadership traits. During my lifetime participating in local churches, and more than 20 years of vocational ministry leadership, I have come to believe that there are at least four primary characteristics in the "DNA" of High Impact Churches:

High Impact Churches are...

Vision-Driven.

Prayer Covered

Faith Filled

Leadership Lifted

Each of these dimensions are synergistic—eliminate one and you weaken the whole. And, while other churches may have one or more of these characteristics present, they do not have all four. When all four of these dimensions are present, high impact ministry happens!

Vision-Driven

A vision helps you see beyond the practical into the possible. When I lived along the coast of California I would occasionally drive home under a thick cover of fog. Fortunately I had driven the road many times. So, while reducing my speed, I continued forward because I knew the way.

Vision-driven churches know with certainty that they are walking the path that God has prepared for them. Vision-driven churches stay the course when the weekly ministry of the church seems difficult. They are engaged at the level of faith, not feelings.

Some people, when thinking about vision, start thinking about ethereal concepts and mystical ruminations. I'm not suggesting that at all. I think that vision from God calls for responsible stewardship of people, resources, and opportunity. In a word, being vision driven is a managed process.

Many leadership theorists have also suggested inherent differences between leadership and management. I think the contrast is overdrawn. Every effective leader I have ever met has also managed well. The key is what you manage. *Effective leaders manage priorities and values rather than focus on activities.* Ken Blanchard sees this clearly when he is quoted in NetFax as saying, "There are two parts to leadership...one is the vision casting and the other is implementation...you have to implement things that match your vision. And remember, the thinking that got you to where you are today, will not get you to where you need to go". (NetFax, Leadership Network, 1-800-765-5323)

VISION QUOTABLES...and my two-cents worth

*Vision is a "realistic, credible, attractive future for your organization" (Nanus, Visionary Leadership, 1992).

If the leader can share the passion that God has placed in their heart and translate that into a vision that the people can see, then High Impact happens!

Vision is "a clear mental image of a preferable future, imparted by God to his chosen servants, based upon an accurate understanding of God, self, and circumstances" (Barna, Without a Vision, the People Perish, 1991).

Vision is not the near psychotic break from reality that many fancy could happen in their lives "if" something changed.
Vision is clear, it comes from God, and is based on the reality of God's calling and His gifts given to us.

"The right vision is an idea so powerful that it literally jump-starts the future by calling forth the energies, talents, and resources to make things happen"(Nanus)

Big vision that comes from God energizes and captures the spirit and imagination of all who are touched by it. My experience shows that over time, visionary leadership draws big vision people.

Prayer Covered

FACING THE SNAKE

Prayer is critical to a high impact church because it is the most spiritually intensive enterprise you will ever engage in! It is "strikingly" similar to Jay Rathman's story:

Jay, a 45-year old seasoned hunter was deer hunting in Northern California. He climbed to a ledge on the slope of a rocky gorge and raised his head to check out the ledge above, when as he puts it:

"I caught a movement to the right of my face. I instinctively pushed myself back and a rattler struck, just missing my right ear." The four-foot snake's fangs got snagged in the neck of Rathman's wool turtleneck sweater, and the force of the strike caused it to land on his left shoulder. It then coiled around his neck. He grabbed it behind the head with his left hand and could feel the warm venom running down the skin of his neck, the rattlers making a furious racket. He fell backwards and slid head first down the steep slope, through brush and lava rocks, his rifle and binoculars bouncing beside him. "As luck would have it," he said in describing the incident to a Department of Fish and Game official, "I ended up wedged between some rocks with my feet caught uphill from my head. I could barely move." He got his right hand on his rifle and used it to disengage the fangs from his sweater, but the snake had enough leverage to strike again. "He made about eight attempts and managed to hit me with his nose just below my eye about four times. I kept my face turned so he couldn't get a good angle with his fangs, but it was very close. This chap and I were eyeball to eyeball and I found out that snakes don't blink."

High Impact Churches often face rattlesnakes. Rattlesnakes don't blink and neither do High Impact Churches when they are certain of the Master's call and covered with prayer.

High Impact Churches thrive with prayer. Prayer has to precede every aspect of the ministry and be cultivated within the ministry as well. Prayer is absolutely necessary because of the spiritual implications of planting a High Impact Church. If the church is going to gain ground for the Gospel in the lives of people, families, and the greater community, you are sure to meet resistance! Each step along the way we have sensed varying measures of resistance in both the visible and invisible realms. Leadership teams who pray together and the cultivation of personal prayer warriors all are essential for vital ministry.

During our experience planting CVC, we have faced many challenges that we believe required intense prayer. At our launch, over 2000 hours a month of prayer occurred by prayer partners outside our community. Just 4 weeks before we were to publicly launch our church, the county leadership gave us (after several months of pleading!) the permission for a temporary occupancy permit in a warehouse. That was a breakthrough! But, it also meant that we had 3 weeks to transform an empty building into a 10,000 square foot worship and children's ministry space. God worked a miracle that many said could not be done through His people and the prevailing power of prayer.

Faith Filled

Establishing a High Impact Church is a faith filled enterprise. Venturing into the unknown where God is leading is a faith driven journey. God led Abram to that journey when He called him to move out to a land that he had not yet seen, to a promise that he had not received, for an inheritance that he would not personally claim. Establishing a High Impact Church can be particularly dangerous in an existing setting. Even unchurched people have recognized the peril in establishing a new order of things:

"There is nothing more difficult to carry out, nor more doubtful of success, nor more dangerous to handle, than to initiate a new order of things. For the reformer has enemies in all who profit by the old order, and only lukewarm defenders in all those who profit by the new order.

This luke-warmness arises partly from fear of their adversaries, who have law in their favor; and partly from the incredulity of mankind, who do not truly believe in anything new until they have actual experience of it"(Machiavelli, The Prince, 1513 A.D.)

While we would not want to lift up Machiavelli as a model (!), however we certainly want High Impact Church leaders to recognize the price to be paid. Particularly for those in an existing situation…recognize the risks! There is no vested interest on the part of many existing leaders to change…in fact it represents a potential loss of power and position. So, go into the process with your eyes open!

Part of the price of faith-filled leadership is to risk moving forward into the unknown. In order to do so with confidence, the leader has to be certain of the vision and clear about the picture ahead. Only when the leader can cast the vision clear enough to see with eyes of faith will people begin to follow into the realm of the uncertain and invisible. Daniel Brown (Pastor of Coastlands Church in Aptos, California) has a helpful insight on this dimension when he says that, "Leadership is cultivating, in people today, a future willingness on their part to follow you into something new for the sake of something great". "Men will never cast off their dearest pleasures upon the dreary request of someone who doesn't ever seem to mean what he says" (Richard Baxter)

Leadership Lifted

Leaders lift High Impact Churches. Plain and simple as can be. Leadership is the difference. "Everything rises and falls on leadership" (John Maxwell). The leader of a High Impact Church recognizes their role of calling forth God's people into His future vision for them. It means identifying the gifts and ministry passions of the people and, like Nehemiah, clarifying the task to be accomplished.

Building shared vision that galvanizes God's people is a mysterious enterprise that results in a sense of awe and camaraderie. When it's right, you know it. But, understanding how to do it in advance can feel a little vague. Of course, the "aha" moment we are all looking for is when we hear a church leader saying to a new friend, "The reason we do _____ here at our church is _____". And, you find them quoting God's vision and His focus that was birthed in your heart as a leader and now is carried on in their heart. At that moment, you want to die and go home to be with Jesus, because you know it's all downhill from there! The bottom line for leaders is they want to lift others into the fulfillment of seeing God use them for His kingdom purposes.

CONVICTIONS OF A FAITH-FILLED HEART

Three convictions that simply must take root in the heart of a High Impact Church Planter are these:

1) <u>Lost people matter to God</u>.... Those of us who spend lots of time "in church" can lose our heart and love for people outside the family of God. God's heart is to reach people and many times a new church can do just that. New churches often are able to cross racial, language, social, and other barriers that have stymied existing churches. I personally do not have the gift of evangelism. And yet, I have come to the place where I am convinced that evangelism must take center stage in the life of the church...it is the one thing that Christians will not do for all eternity! Evangelism, if not prioritized, tends to drift south in the church priority list. So, the passion to reach lost people must become real for the church leadership and become a matter of personal priority.

2) <u>Church planting is God's tool for this hour</u>. Several researchers suggest that a new church reaches one new person for every 10 people already involved. An existing church often requires more than 100 people to reach one new person! FOCUS is the key...new churches must reach new people or they die! Existing churches sometimes fool themselves into thinking that "maintenance" is the goal. If you are being led to plant a church, then you must be prepared to pay the price and confront the lethargy of your own soul to give birth to the new ministry. God will guide you in the birthing process and your new work will enlarge the kingdom!

3) <u>Our culture requires re-engineered ministry with a faithful message</u>. In a "post-Christian" era like ours, every church must become a "new church". People today are very interested in spiritual things and they simply don't care about denominations and church quarrels. Each church has the opportunity to recapture the sense of being a "mission station" to reach those in its community. We must be willing to change ANY method as long as we do not change the message of God's great love for the world around us. Faith filled leaders and churches see God reaching lost people through any method that doesn't compromise the message

35

A High Impact Church will consistently exhibit all four of the characteristics discussed in this lesson. A vision-driven, prayer-covered, faith-filled and leadership lifted ministry will impact its community in a dynamic way!

KEY TRANSFERABLE CONCEPTS:

Vision drives High Impact Churches. Only when you "begin with the end" in mind can you evaluate the structure, systems, and strategies of your ministry

Prayer must cover each aspect of High Impact Ministry. It is clear that prayer warriors from outside your local context will "set the pace" for your High Impact Ministry.

Leaders of High Impact Churches are faith-filled. Only when leaders engage the God given vision with faith can they see God's hand at work. Everything rises and falls on leadership. Leaders in High Impact Ministry recognize their roles in lifting the ministry environment and ministry leaders across the entire church

High Impact Churches are committed to becoming large churches from the beginning. Because they "begin with the end in mind" they think, strategize, structure, and behave with the mindset of a large church from the first days of ministry development. Growth barriers are more easily broken when the vision and faith for barrier breaking are present at day one.

SELF STUDY ACTIVITIES:

Activity One: Bible Study and Application

Churches sometimes face obstacles that simply refuse to budge. Many times, the only way obstacles are overcome is through intense prayer.

Read Mark 9:14-29

How do you suppose the disciples had tried to drive out the demon? Why were they unable to drive it out? (see verses 28-29 note: some manuscripts say "by prayer and fasting" in verse 29)

What areas of your life and ministry do you think are crying out for more intensely focused prayer?

Open your calendar and talk with God about when you might schedule some intentional prayer (and possibly fasting) about these areas.

Activity Two:

Many churches are planted in part out of a frustration with the status quo or an existing church's inability to flex quickly to change in vision or emphasis. Why would a new church be able to deal more effectively with these issues?

Whether you are a church planter or a leader in an existing church, what spiritual qualities must be developed in your people in order to cultivate an ability to flex with changing power and position?

Activity Three:

Watch for people in your church or ministry who have been led well— people who can communicate to others the reasons why your ministry does what it does each week.

What is it about these people that allow them to "get it?"

What is it about their leader that got the message across in such an effective manner?

Chapter 5
A new paradigm for Church Planting:
Possessed by God's vision

In our own church plant, we had been meeting for just a few weeks with a small core group of about 35 people. Friends of one of our core families came to visit from out of the area to see how the church planting was going. Following our core gathering, the friend commented, "Man, you guys are really sold out to this aren't you? You don't have a plan 'B, do you?" You know, he was right! Each of us believed that not only had we seen God's vision, it had possessed us!

During my time as a staff member, pastor, denominational leader, and founding church planter, I have observed key leadership principles— principles that help to determine whether a high impact church leader and team will be able to sustain fruitful, barrier-breaking ministry over time. *Perhaps the key characteristic of fruitful high impact leaders is that they are radically possessed by God's vision.*

The prophet Isaiah speaks of vision in a somewhat surprising way:

"Therefore I said, "Turn away from me; let me weep bitterly. Do not try to console me over the destruction of my people." The Lord, the LORD Almighty, has a day of tumult and trampling and terror in the Valley of Vision, a day of battering down walls and of crying out to the mountains." (Isaiah 22: 4-5)

When I first discovered this text, I was fascinated. I've always thought of vision coming from the mountaintops. After a long reflective retreat in the peaceful serenity of the mountaintop, then vision can come. And yet God told Isaiah that a tumult, trampling, and terror would come in the Valley of Vision. That rang a bell! So many times in my life and ministry, the context for vision has been a bruised, battered, and broken state of mind and heart. *Only when I was ready to let go of everything could God give me everything.* Vision possesses you when you are absolutely clear about the source of the vision and able to receive it in full measure; it very well may not come until you are in the valley.

In my experience and study, I have discerned several characteristics of a godly vision for a high impact church. A high impact vision will encompass each of the following characteristics:

1) Challenges "Growth Barriers"

High Impact Churches are ready to challenge the typical barriers that exist within church life and within the community where they live and breathe. High Impact Churches look for ways around, through, or over barriers that are placed in the pathway of fulfilling God's vision for ministry.

Barriers exist at various growth levels. High Impact Church leaders must recognize those barriers at each level and work to remove and overcome those barriers. Some of the most common barriers that have been identified include:

* 200 barrier: This is the challenge of transitioning the pastoral/chaplain style church environment to a ranching and outreach mindset. We think the keys to breaking through this barrier are to cultivate and model a contagious desire to grow, identify growth accelerators, teach and explain the pastoral transition from shepherd to rancher, and deal with small church mentality by focusing outward! High Impact Church Leaders offer leadership and lay ministry training to equip a team of leaders.

Because of our model for launching a High Impact Church, we believe that this barrier can be broken immediately at the *first public worship service. High Impact churches "begin with the end in mind".* At CVC, we structured and taught our people in order to break these first two barriers in our hearts and mind even before we began the first worship service.

* 400 barrier: This size church must move from a lay-led model to a staff led model. Key steps include assisting the leadership base to understand the need for key staffing resources, to transition the pastor into a leadership role rather than manager of machinery, to align resources with vision, and to restructure the governance model towards vision fulfillment and away from machinery management. In our early days, we operated with a staff led ministry model even when we couldn't afford to pay virtually anyone! Ministry leaders were all treated like staff and given both the responsibility and authority to carry out their ministry roles.

* 800 barrier: Challenges at this level are both systemic and cultural. In other words, establishing systems to meet specific needs and changing the culture of the ministry are critical barrier breakers. Specific tasks include elevating the thinking of the pastor, hiring exceptional staff for ministry excellence, creation of multiple entry points, and assimilation and discipleship systems via small groups/classes. Providing care for the enlarged group through the "one anothers" of the New Testament is the critical systemic challenge.

Our own church has benefited from the notion of "BHAG's" (Big Holy Audacious Goals) made popular by James Collins and Jerry Porras in their book, Built to Last (though they envisioned "hairy" rather than "holy" goals). The ministry we started began with outlandish goals. We felt they were a natural byproduct of God's vision. Other people thought they were foolish. Over time however, they helped create in people a sense of anticipation at how God could break through barriers of faith or fact.

CVC Goals
(updated 8/99 after only 18 months in ministry!)

Because God has seen fit to exceed what was apparently our smallish understanding of His vision for this ministry, we have revised our goals as follows:

Original Goal: Reach 1000 Adults in weekend worship within 5 years of our first public worship service
Revised Goal: Reach 5000 people in weekend worship services by he 5th birthday of our public launch (February, 2003)

Original Goal: Have a minimum of 20 acres of property, with worship center seating capacity of 1000
Revised Goal: 40 acre campus with worship center seating capacity of 2000 by 7th birthday

Original Goal: 40% of those attending worship be previously unchurched

Original Goal: 50% of those attending weekend worship using spiritual gifts for ministry, involved in a small group, and have completed personal discipleship training

Original Goal: Plant one new church per year after five years
Revised Goal: Partner in planting 5 new churches per year via leadership, finances, or internships

---

2) Challenges People

High Impact churches rally people to something greater than the norm. They challenge existing benchmarks and move the bar up. Because of the faith and vision of the founding leadership team, there is a propensity to attract others who want to see big things accomplished for God. The Prime Minister of France once said, "If you are doing big things, you attract big people. If you are doing little things, you attract little people". It may sound harsh, but our experience has certainly mirrored this truth.

In our High Impact Church, we are also learning how to challenge people on the journey itself. During our first two years of life, we probably under-challenged people on the specific roles and responsibilities that came with leading a church. We were focused at fulfilling our vision to see people come to know Christ and grow in their relationship with Him. As time goes on, we have become ever more certain that God was bringing people specifically to us to help fulfill the vision for ministry. As Wayne Cordeiro of New Hope Chapel in Oahu says, "Everyone is a 10 somewhere". Finding that somewhere is your challenge as a leader! Discovering where people are a "10" and connecting them to that ministry is our increasing passion.

Part of the effectiveness in our challenging people was having a clear vision of where we were going and how we were going to get there. Alvin Toffler, the author of Future Shock, said, "You've got to think about big things while you're doing small things, so that all the small things go in the right direction". Our articulation of a clear plan prior to establishing the ministry was a touchstone for us that enabled people to have confidence in our vision and direction.

3) Challenges "Conventional Thinking"

High Impact churches are ready not only to break through growth barriers, but they challenge conventional thinking at every turn. The four most common "stinking thinking" barriers High Impact Churches challenge are:

a) "New churches are small"

High Impact Churches start with a passion to reach large groups of people for Christ. In so doing, they refuse to believe that they are constricted as to size, space, or scope of outreach. Just as Rick Warren's initial vision for Saddleback Church (see Purpose Driven Church) served as an inspiration to me personally, so a vision for growing ministries helps High Impact Churches move beyond a "small is of God" mentality.

b) "New churches do not have (or really need) resources"

Many existing churches are hesitant to help new churches because they are uncertain of their potential for success. New churches themselves also often feel a poverty of spirit because of the many baby believers in their midst. High Impact Churches believe that God provides resources through all of His people. Family, friends, other church colleagues, Christians who join the challenge of a new work, and new believers all have potential and unlimited resources to share with the larger vision. God will never impart His vision without providing His resources through all of His people.

c) "New churches can't..."

The wall of impossibility exists for all churches. For High Impact Churches, the wall of impossibility exists, but it is not permanent. New ministries that need to be launched, new groups of people that need to be reached, and new methods of sharing the gospel all stand as opportunities to see God at work. Rather than hearing "can't", High Impact Churches hear "must".

d) "New churches aren't needed"

I can't count the number of times we heard that when we started our church in Carson Valley, Nevada. We regularly received phone calls from people saying "Why would you start a church here? Everyone here already goes to church" (this in a community with only 5% churched!). Existing churches often wrestle with the effort and energy required to start a new church. In light of their existing circumstances, starting a new endeavor seems beyond the realm of reasonableness.

And yet, as we stated before, the Great Commission compels us to reach the unreached. According to the American Society for Church Growth, there is no county in America more churched today than 10 years ago. High Impact Churches are needed in virtually every community in America!

4) Challenges "Status Quo"

High Impact Churches recognize the law of inertia and confront it head on. People, new churches, and life in general tend towards stagnation. High Impact Churches and leaders regularly address the needs within their community by modeling at least these key behaviors:

* *Prepare in advance and communicate to people about the future.* Regularly casting vision as a leader is a must!

* *Model commitment to keep moving.* "He who stands still will be trampled by the herd of retreating rhinos!" Paul's example in Philippians 3 where he describes, "pressing on for the upward call of God in Christ Jesus" is what we want to model.

* *Fight against entropy!* Keep persistent in execution of your vision strategy. Our persistent focus on our monthly Discovery classes has enabled us to keep people moving forward.

Let people see what you are aiming for! In our own setting we did "preview" services before launch; we then were able to let people "see and feel" what we were aiming at. We have regularly used high quality resources (Injoy, Willow Creek, Saddleback) as vehicles for people to dream beyond the present.

5) Preceded by Prayer

Our own High Impact Church, Carson Valley Christian Center, had about 2000 hours of prayer each week at its launch. We had Faith Promise Partners, early members, pastors, and whole groups of people in existing churches supporting us through the ministry of prayer. Throughout our young life we have witnessed great prayer moments.

Some of these great prayer moments came as we faced a critical need. Even more of them came as an attendee would risk asking a friend to church. People would gather around and pray. Many times a new birth would take place on that first exposure to the church. People have often said, "I've been waiting all my life to find God and your church was started just for me!"

6) Emboldened by the Holy Spirit

High Impact Churches are distinctive movements of God in the heart of a leader, in an emerging body of believers, and in an unreached community of seekers. None of the vision, plans, strategies, or activities will bear any lasting fruit unless the Holy Spirit moves the ministry forward. "Unless the LORD builds the house, its builders labor in vain." Psalm 127:1a (NIV)

We have regularly challenged ourselves by asking the question, "If we knew we could not fail, what would we do for the glory of God?" Because the greatest churches in the kingdom of God have yet to be planted, High Impact leaders submit themselves to the Holy Spirit's direction and empowerment as they envision God's future for themselves and for their ministries. We recognize that it was the Holy Spirit's direction and His strength that emboldened us to seize new territory for the sake of kingdom.

Leaders possessed by God's vision for high impact ministry will be energized and refreshed by the sight of God working in their midst again and again to accomplish the vision He's given. High impact leaders who dare to raise up Big Holy Audacious Goals for their people will be able to sustain fruitful, barrier-breaking ministry over time. This is the inheritance of those possessed by a God "who is able to do immeasurably more than all we ask or imagine, according to his power that is at work within us...to him be glory in the church and in Christ Jesus throughout all generations, for ever and ever! Amen." Ephesians 3:20-21(NIV)

KEY TRANSFERABLE CONCEPTS:

High Impact Church Leaders are "possessed" by God's vision for ministry. Because of this, High Impact Church Leaders do ministry as a "conviction" not a convenience."

High Impact Churches challenge barriers. Understanding the people, social, and cultural barriers and challenging them is key to High Impact ministry.

SELF STUDY ACTIVITIES:

Activity One:

Which numerical growth barrier does your church face? What specific action plan would you implement to break through that barrier? Outline your barrier and your plan. Show it to a mentor and discuss.

Activity Two:

When did you last talk with someone who held the "small is of God" philosophy of church ministry? What textual support did he or she use? How did you respond?

Activity Three: Bible Study and Application

Paul: A man possessed by God's vision
Read the following passages and use them to help you answer the questions in #2, below. (Feel free to explore passages of your own choosing as well.)

Acts 9:15-16
Romans 15:15-21
Galatians 1:15-24
Galatians 2:6-9
Ephesians 3:7-9

Colossians 1:24-29
1 Timothy 2:7
2 Timothy 4:16-17

How would you define Paul's vision for ministry? From whom did he receive his vision? What was his focus, his target group? What challenges to his vision did he face, from both inside and outside the Church? What gave him the strength to hold to his vision in the face of opposition?

3. What encouragement and lessons can you gain for your   own vision and ministry in light of Paul's example?

Chapter 6
Starting a New Work:
11 Strategic Steps in the Journey

During the first years of Carson Valley Christian Center, various people jumped into our ministry to spur us on at strategic moments. Don Nelson is an ordained minister and friend of mine. He helped our church to establish our "First Touch" ministry, which helps people feel welcome to CVC, and has since gone on to another new church to help them with their launching process. Don has spent time in established churches and now in two successful new church plants. He makes the following observation about what he calls *"New Church Physics"*:

"It's not different math, it is different physics. An existing church has inertia (and like the force of gravity, it has to be broken). New churches have no mass, are not at rest. They are in motion, and a little force moves them. A new church sucks other objects into it as it moves. The spiritual, emotional, cultural physics are different."

New Church Physics are at play in the starting of a High Impact Church. But to achieve the inertia-defying properties desired the following 11 strategic steps should be followed to start a High Impact Church:

Step 1: Uphold a clear and well processed, prayed for vision.

This vision has to be prayed through and painstakingly shared with successive groups of people who will join your team. Because High Impact Churches reach large groups of people early on, it is essential to have a clear vision that you know comes from the throne of God. If you don't have a clear idea of what to do with the crowd when it comes, you will be in trouble!

Step 2: Lay out an aggressive plan of action, including a fundraising plan.

There are some tremendous resources on the market to help you with developing your action plan. Four of my favorites are:

Purpose Driven Church Planting Materials (www.purposedriven.com)

Dynamic Church Planting (Paul Becker, 619-749-9347)

Church Planter's Toolkit (Bob Logan & Steve Ogne, Church Resource Ministries)

Planting Thriving New Churches (Ray Johnston, www.baysideonline.com)

In my own consulting experience, *I have found that church planters tend to underestimate the amount of money that will be required to successfully plant a High Impact Church. But they overestimate the amount that a denominational agency, mother church, or sponsor should be obligated to give them at launch.* If you are a High Impact Church leader, people whom you have impacted in ministry will support your vision. Raise funds from those who "buy in" to your vision based on God's working in their lives.

Step 3: Create a "people pathway" for assimilation.

Assimilation at every level of involvement revolves around connecting people in relationships and in ministry service. I have found Rick Warren's model at Saddleback to be the most helpful in our setting. (See *The Purpose Driven Church*, specifically "Part Five: Building Up the Church.") We have since changed our visual paradigm (Rather than use a 4 stage baseball diamond, I say we aren't as smart as Saddleback, so we use a triangle with the words Attract, Attach, and Activate), but the models of those who have gone before us were tremendously helpful. Articulating a clear plan at the start helped people to have confidence about where we were heading and connecting them in relationships and ministry.

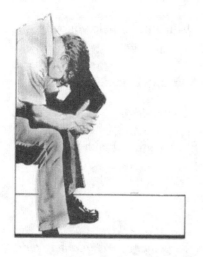

The Key Process Question....

Can you take a New Believer through the Spiritual Journey to Leadership?

Over time we have "morphed" our own ministry structures in order to focus on "Visitors", "Attenders" and "Leaders". Assimilation is different at each numerical level, but still revolves around connecting people in relationships and ministry.

Step 4: Make your church planting plans flexible and be open to unexpected opportunities.

We had some great plans on paper. Some of them even worked. Others didn't. We recorded thirteen 60-second commercials for radio. We got zero response. Direct mailing in our area didn't prove to be nearly as effective as we hoped. But, we did discover some great strategies that did fit our area.

Local public access television is actually watched here! We also found that newspaper inserts here reach 80% of all households in the area. The cost was substantially cheaper than direct mail and we found that people retained the inserts, sometimes for months.

My brother Gene is a marketing genius and many of our early inserts are classics! We took some flak from Christians in the area, but got a very positive response from the unchurched community. We took the flak and God built the flock.

Step 5: Prayerfully seek godly core leaders and key ministry leaders.

Implosion is a critical danger to High Impact Church ministry. Churches that attract crowds and don't have the leadership base to effectively minister will be handicapped from the start. Seeking godly core leaders as part of your launch team and cultivating a game plan for how the church will "go public" with specific ministries is a MUST for a successful launch of your High Impact Church.

Step 6: Hold preview services 3-6 months prior to your launch service. Build your core to 100 adults or more.

At each preview service we tried to approximate musical style, children's ministry, and teaching that we felt we could attain by Launch Sunday (yes, a huge step of faith). We challenged people who attended the Preview Services to receive Christ as Savior and to consider becoming part of the CVC Launch Team. Each preview service added 20 or more people to our launch team!

Step 7: Engage people in Ministries, Discovery classes, Small groups and Bible studies.

After each preview service, we continued to help people move through the bases. We even offered Discovery 101 the same afternoon as the preview services. In hindsight, this was a great move. People who were energized by the Sunday morning program would come out of curiosity to 101. There, I had the chance to explain the basics of the Gospel and to share the CVC vision.

The 5 months leading up to our own public launch (September-January) were high-energy intensive with people being connected to ministries, Discovery classes, and small groups. This period was a key to the success of our launch and we strongly advocate taking enough time to do it well. During this entire period, we did receive an offering each week from our core and committed people because it is one of our ten key values.

Step 8: Identify the core group as your "Launch Team"; create job descriptions and prepare for launch.

By the time we launched, we had specific roles identified and a key sense of what it would take to start our High Impact Church. *When we actually launched, 65 of our 100 adults had been through Discovery 301 and were serving in ministry on the date of our birth.* We set the pattern at the beginning and it is now firmly embedded in our DNA. A copy of the actual Launch Team Roles from our launch team is included in the appendix of resources to this book.

Step 9: Create excellent publicity, especially 2 months before launch...

As I've mentioned, my brother Gene is a marketing whiz. He believes strongly in what I call "bread crumb" advertising. He builds a game plan where over a 3-6 week period we build public interest and drive them to a specific response. In our case, we built a theme, "The Next Great Day in History" that moved people to focus on February 22, 1998. Then, the second segment focused on the teaching series entitled, "Winning Big in the Game of Life" (4 Tape Series available from VisionQuest Ministries for $15 at Box 275, Genoa, NV 89411)

We involved our people in the process by giving them fold-over wallet sized cards and encouraging them to canvass neighborhoods and local businesses. The expectation is to create a "buzz" of activity in your area. When we launched, we think we created a "big event" mentality. Not only is event evangelism right in the center of our vision, we believe that it is right for our area. George Barna believes that as many as 40% of the people who visit your church do so through a special event. The launch of your High Impact Church is the most important event in your early life and will determine the trajectory of the next 12-24 months.

Step 10: Plan a super launch and go public with the key things you'd die for.

You can't control everything. Mistakes happen. Weather gets bad. People get sick. But, you can decide what you are "going to the wall" for. In our case, we decided that we would focus on three things:

1) Relevant Biblical Messages
2) Upbeat Contemporary Music
3) Excellent Children's Ministry

These three program distinctives have remained our "crowd" focus to this day. We built our launch as big as possible. We have 100,000 people in our 30-mile focus area, so in hindsight, we got about 0.5% of our target population to attend our launch. Almost 4 years later, we now have over 1% of our target population attending each week. How you start impacts you more than you can imagine.

Begin well!

Step 11: Go for it! Affirm Philippians 4:13 and practice "Continuous Improvement."

God is sovereign. It is His church. You are accountable for gifts and resources He has entrusted to you. But, He is the one who causes the growth. God will do way beyond your imagination and you will see 30-60-100 fold return from your sowing of His seed. Spend lots of time affirming your leadership team. Be a positive person from the platform and practice "continuous improvement". Build a culture of affirmation AND expectation. God is good...all the time! All the time...God is good!

Conclusion

Church ought to be the most exciting place on earth. My prayer is that as you move ahead with the eleven steps we've outlined in this lesson, you will discover the exciting dynamics of "New Church Physics and your High Impact Church will become the place to be in your community!

KEY TRANSFERABLE CONCEPTS:

High Impact Churches "begin with the end in mind". They have a plan and they are strategic about their plan.

High Impact Churches are structured for leaders. From the beginning, High Impact Churches draw leaders, equip leaders, and release leaders for ministry

High Impact Churches see "marketing" as a vehicle for creating awareness. Marketing brings very few people to church. However, it creates a climate where people who are invited can connect their invitation with a positive perception that has already been developed.

SELF STUDY ACTIVITIES:

Activity One: Research your Community

What means of publicity are most effective in your area (Radio, Direct Mailing, Public Access Television, Newspaper Inserts, Other)? Ask local business owners as well as churches about types of publicity they've tried as well as specific results. How will your findings influence your plans to publicize your ministry?

Which community events are well attended in your area? What does your community enjoy? Research community events and attend them with a focus on understanding what makes your area tick. (Remember not to limit your attendance to events you personally enjoy—include popular events you may not enjoy to get a more well-rounded picture of what your community is like and what it attends.)

Activity Two: Fundraising Plans

As the leader in a church, you are the chief fundraiser. List out possible avenues of resource cultivation in your existing or future ministry.

Activity Three: Building your Library

Visit the following websites. Investigate the resources offered by each ministry and which might be most helpful to you.

www.purposedriven.com (Purpose Driven resources from Saddleback)
www.barna.org (Barna Research Online)
www.dcpi.org (Dynamic Church Planting International)
www.crmnet.org (Church Resource Ministries)

Activity Four: Bible Study and Application

Read Luke 14:28-32 In these parables, Jesus is discussing the cost of becoming his disciple. However, there are principles to be gleaned here as well in the area of looking ahead to the desired goal and making sure that the resources are available to reach that goal. Pray through the passage, thinking about your own ministry context as well as the steps outlined in this lesson. What resources stand ready and available for you? What resources still need to be marshaled before you head into battle?

Chapter 7
Up Close and Personal

High Impact Church Planting is gut-wrenching, time-consuming, ulcer-producing work that should strike fear into the hearts of those called to do it. It requires "guts" that some days you might not want to muster, it requires time and energy you might not want to give, and it exacts a toll on its leaders that you might not want to pay. Sure, there will be moments that make your heart sing; just as certain, however, is the fact that there will be moments that make your heart sick.

We believe that what God calls you to do, He enables you to do by the power of his Spirit. But that does not mean you will not break a sweat. During our first three years of starting and leading a High Impact Church, we have understood some specific challenges of the ministry we believe are critical. It sometimes feels like the goal of the adversary is to "knock you off your horse". Here are several areas where the ministry challenges get "up close and personal" for key leaders in High Impact Church Planting:

Your Spouse & Family

All ministry makes demands on family. Starting a High Impact Church makes those demands a little bit more expansive. Because High Impact Churches start with a committed core and then quickly draw a crowd, the demands on time and developing relationships are extensive. Persons who tend towards work and family imbalances will find High Impact Church life a potentially seductive temptress. As a lifelong recovering workaholic, I have battled the workload of our growing church from the start. In the early days, I was desperate for something to happen. As time went on, I became equally desperate for things to take a break! We are convinced that a healthy marriage and clear communication about expectations for the children are essential.

For example, healthy communication in the marriage of the HICP leaders is essential, and required for the work. If spouses are not on the same page, then the relationship will erode, and the ministry will suffer. Weaknesses in the marriages of the leadership team will be replicated in the lives and marriages of those they mentor and lead. Conversely, strong marriages among the leadership team will help to cultivate a climate of strong and growing marriages among new leaders and in the congregation.

Likewise, appropriate communication should take place with children. Our children have had to make some specific adjustments that required delicate direction on our part as parents. As a practical example, our oldest daughter was 13 when we first moved to start our church. Because we came from a large church, we wanted our daughter to continue to be part of a dynamic Youth Ministry. For 10 months after our arrival, our daughter participated in the youth ministry of an existing local solid church. When it was time for CVC to have its own youth ministry, she made the change to our own youth group. Because she knew it was coming (we had talked about it from the beginning), she was able to navigate the transition with relative ease.

Your Staff Team

If clear communication between married partners is critical to the church's health, then likewise clear communication of expectations is essential for your staff team. As the size of the church increases, the ability to identify, equip, and facilitate reproduction of leadership is fundamental to church health. Clearly your staff/program leaders (whether paid or volunteer) are the first link in this chain.

Taking care of your key leadership team by supporting them with prayer, strengthening them with equipping, and surrounding them with positive ministry models is central to the High Impact Church leadership challenge. If your leaders do not know what level of commitment is expected from them, or how much time their ministry will realistically take, then you are doing a disservice to them and their families. Also, if you are failing to pray for their families on a regular basis, then you are failing them. We have strived to develop a healthy key leadership team from the beginning.

"There are 3 kinds of people in the world—Those who don't know what's happening, Those who watch what is happening, Those who make things happen" (Nicholas Butler, Former President of Columbia University).

Leadership begins with self-leadership, so we want to better equip people to become effective leaders in their lives and ministries. As a matter of personal spiritual discipline, I pray for the marriages and children of each of our staff members. This has been an important discipline in our setting as we live and minister in a state where divorce is an economic commodity (under the "right" circumstances, you can get divorced in Nevada in 72 hours!). Because of the carnage around us, we have worked particularly hard to insure that our marriages remain stable.

I am a constant reader, so I regularly share resources with our staff team and our team has developed that habit with one another. In addition, we have made it a point to visit two or three larger churches each year and meet with their staff teams. This has been a tremendous benefit, not only in what we have learned (and shared with the churches we visited), but in the bonding that takes place during our trips. This "benchmarking" helps us as we are exposed to ministry models to stimulate our reflection and thinking. Frankly, we "borrow" good ideas from all over the country!

Our staff team has also worked on being a learning community and valuing learning that is for the head, for the heart, and for the spirit. If we are not clear about what God is saying in us and among us, then it will be hard for us to teach our people about God's pathway for them to follow. We have been developing our ability to work together as a team and cultivating our sense of shared mission and vision. This develops slowly, but certainly; if you have enough vision casting, motivation, shared experiences and time together, it will develop in your midst. We currently are scheduling a staff/spouses gathering quarterly and two extended staff retreats annually.

We also do everything in our power to "hire for heartbeat". We certainly want to have competent and capable people on our staff team. But, our experience over time suggests that hiring for passion and fit are ultimately of greater value than competency alone. Several friends in ministry have been particularly helpful in modeling that ministry value.

Leadership

The vision will always be "up for grabs" in the mind of some. No matter how clearly you communicate and articulate the vision, someone will try to change it. *You will face a leadership challenge in starting a High Impact Church.* Count on it. Typically it will come from a person with leadership experience in an established church. At first, all the things different about your new church will attract them. But, slowly and surely they will wonder why you don't focus, prioritize, or conduct yourself in the same way as they believe church should be done. In some ways, it is like the experience of many young couples early in their marriage ("I'll marry him/her and THEN, I'll change them").

In our case, we faced specific leadership challenges repeatedly during the first two years. In each and every case, the leaders started with CVC by stating that "God had brought CVC to our area". They were enthused about the vision and excited about the fruitfulness. But, that enthusiasm soon faded into subtle and then specific criticisms of how we should be more like their prior ministry settings. In the end, many of the "churched" people we attracted in the first year left CVC with disappointment. Corporately, our struggle was with the loss of people who had gifts that could have been used to minister to unchurched people. But, we had a choice to make and we are glad we maintained our vision.

Stay the course! If you have gone through the 11 strategic steps we outlined and you are certain of God's vision then don't sell out on it! Don't allow God's working in your heart to be bought out or sabotaged by a self-appointed reformer. God will bring many people alongside you to help in your ministry. Discern those who have a passion for God's work and share your vision. Listen to them. However, some who come alongside you were not sent from God. Let them drift away or send them away if need be. Strong language, I know. But, lots of new churches get "hijacked" by misguided leaders; don't let yours be one of them.

Teaching

It will probably happen in the first six months. It might take a couple of years. But *you will face a Teaching Challenge.* Count on it. When CVC started, we had frustrated people at both ends of the spiritual spectrum believing that we were the answer to the spiritual "drought" in the area. The problem was, if we had fulfilled all their hopes and dreams, we would have been a schizophrenic church with a massive case of multiple personalities!

God called us to certain style of ministry, and gave the senior teaching leader a set of Biblical convictions. We have remained true to those convictions, sometimes at great cost. Wonderfully gifted leaders who did not share our Biblical convictions had to be released to other ministries. New churches are by nature leadership intensive, so each leader that went on to another ministry felt like a leader lost to the vision of CVC. What we have learned however is that God never allows a void in leadership. He always will fill it with people who share the heartbeat for the ministry.

The Financial Cost

Establishing and maintaining a high impact ministry always costs more than you anticipate (somewhat like building a new home). The financial struggles are always more painful, personal, and plentiful than you'd ever think possible. We have found this to be one of the most tangible arenas of our faith journey. It is risky and it has often been VERY difficult. Likewise, the intangible costs for staff and key leaders are huge, in terms of time, energy, and resources.

Our encouragement to you is this: count the cost, and go for it! In the tragic events surrounding the terrorist events on September 11, 2001 several stories of heroism have come forth. One such story surrounds Christian Todd Beamer, singled out by the President in a speech before a joint session of Congress. This believer spoke from an airplane to an airline operator about the terrorists, prayed with her, and was heard later saying, "O.K., let's roll." Several churches have adopted this activist pattern: "Let's pray, let's roll". Because God is a God of active love for those lost, we should be about our Father's business, giving focused attention to those outside God's kingdom.

Living in the Land of Big Dreams

This book, if nothing else, has been an invitation to dream big dreams for God—and to begin living in the land of those dreams, watching them become realities. There are formidable dangers in the land, to be sure, and they are not to be trifled with. But neither are they to be overly feared. He who called you is faithful; and ultimately, there is no safer or more joyful place to live than in the center of God's big dream for you.

In our own life, we will continue to live out and breathe the story that God is writing at Carson Valley Christian Center. If God is birthing in you a heartbeat for High Impact Ministry, then we'd love to hear from you! If you go through the process of starting a High Impact Church, we'd love to hear the story of how God works in your vision to produce a harvest that is 30-60-100 fold.

We have included an appendix with a number of documents and forms that we think might be helpful for your ministry. If you use them and improve them, please share the improved version with us!

We are yours for the kingdom. Seeing a life change, transforming a family, and impacting a community for the cause of Christ are worth the investment of your life!

KEY TRANSFERABLE CONCEPTS:

High Impact Church Planting is costly. Count the cost for your family, your potential staff team, and your key leaders

High Impact Church Planting leaders "begin with the end in mind". Have a clear view of your philosophy of ministry and your teaching foundation so that the ministry can resist the "hijacking" efforts of well intentioned people

High Impact Church Planting is the most dangerous and the most exciting enterprise you'll ever do. Dream a "God-sized" dream, pull up the anchor, and set sail towards the horizon God has for you!

SELF STUDY ACTIVITIES:

Activity One: Family Survey

Take each member of your family (spouse and children) out separately on a date. Use your time together to ask them to share with you honestly about:

The impact they see your current ministry and future ministry plans having on them in particular.

The impact they see your current ministry and future ministry plans having on the family as a whole.

You may want to develop more specific questions relating to your particular ministry context or plans, and adapt those questions to the specific ages and concerns of your family members. (WARNING: Do not use this time to try to address or shoot down any concerns raised. Use this time to listen and your later prayer times. How might God want you to minister differently or relate to your family differently based on the answers you received?)

Activity Two: Staff Cultivation

A. If you have not done so already, create a list (or use whatever format works best for you) of the names of each of your potential staff members, their spouses, and their children. Develop a plan (and implement it) to cover your staff marriages and families with prayer.

What are the best ministry books or resources you've read over the past few months? Have you shared them with key staff members? If not, do so.

Plan a field trip for your staff team to visit a larger church and meet with its staff team. This will stimulate your team's reflection and thinking, as well as aid in knitting your team together to fuel

Activity Three: Bible Study and Application

Up Close and Personal with God

Read Hebrews 4:12-16 Pray that God's word would be living and active today in your heart.

Recognizing that nothing is hidden from God's sight, including the thoughts and attitudes of your heart, ask God to reveal to you your weaknesses and sins in the areas of:

Your relationship with your Spouse and Family
Your relationship with your Staff Team
Your relationship with your Congregation
Your relationship with Finances

Pray through these areas, confessing any sins and weaknesses and taking them to the throne of grace with confidence, asking for God's mercy and grace to work in your heart in these realms.

With God, develop some first growth steps to take in these areas. The joy of living in the land of big dreams can only be fully tasted by those with growing hearts and clear consciences in the realms you've been praying through.

EPILOGUE

Please send stories of how God has used "High Impact Church Planting" or requests for additional materials to:

VisionQuest Ministries
Box 275
Genoa, NV 89411

In the appendix that follows, we have included a number of different types of materials that may be helpful to you in your church or in a church plant. PLEASE do not attempt to just "adopt" them into your setting. ADAPT everything, but make sure it is GOD'S VISION and not mine or yours!

God Bless You!

APPENDIX OF CVC RESOURCES

BYLAWS OF THE
CARSON VALLEY CHRISTIAN CENTER, INC.

This church shall be known as the Carson Valley Christian Center, incorporated under the laws of the State of Nevada.

PURPOSE

Carson Valley Christian Center (CVC) exists to see non Christians become disciples of Jesus Christ

Carson Valley Christian Center will dynamically....

...exalt Jesus, the Light of the World
...equip believers to walk in the Light
...encourage one another to share the Light

STATEMENT OF FAITH

Scripture

We believe that the Bible is the Word of God, fully inspired and without error in the original manuscripts, written under the inspiration of the Holy Spirit, and that it has supreme authority in all matters of faith and conduct (II Timothy 3:16-17).

DR. JOHN JACKSON

The Trinity

We believe that there is one living God, and that He has revealed Himself in three distinct persons: God the Father; God the Son, and God the Holy Spirit (Titus 3:4-6).

a) God the Father: We believe in God the Father: an infinite, personal spirit, perfect in holiness, wisdom, power and love. We believe that He concerns Himself mercifully in the affairs of man, and that He saves from sin and death all that come to Him through Jesus Christ.

b) God the Son: We believe that Jesus Christ is fully God and fully man. He is eternal and shares all of the attributes of deity with the Father and the Holy Spirit, as God's only begotten Son. He was conceived by the Holy Spirit to be born of a virgin, Mary. We believe in His virgin birth, sinless life, miracles and teachings. We believe in His substitutionary atoning death, bodily resurrection, and ascension into Heaven, perpetual intercession for His people and personal, visible return to earth.

c) God the Holy Spirit: We believe that the Holy Spirit is a person and shares all the attributes of deity with the Father and the Son. He came forth from the Father and the Son to convict the world of sin, righteousness and judgment, and to regenerate, sanctify, and empower all who believe in Jesus Christ, and that He is an abiding Helper, Teacher, and Guide.

Salvation

We believe that all men are sinners by nature and by choice and are, therefore, deserving of eternal condemnation. We believe that those who repent of their sins and trust in Jesus Christ as Lord and Savior are regenerated and become children of God by the Holy Spirit (John 1:12, Romans 5:6-8).

The Church

We believe that the Church is the Body of Christ, of which Christ is the Head. It consists of all regenerated persons. We believe in local churches as visible manifestations of the invisible Body of Christ, the Church Universal. We believe that God has given the task of evangelism of the world to the Church under the direction of the Holy Spirit and the Word of God (Acts 1:8, I Corinthians 12:12-14, Ephesians 1:22).

Christian Living

We believe that a Christian should live for the glory of God and the well being of others. Believers are called to live holy and godly lives (I Corinthians 10:31, I Peter 1:5-6, Matthew 22:37-40).

Ordinances

We believe that ordinances of the New Testament church are communion (the Lord's Supper) and water baptism for believers by immersion as a public act of confession of faith(Acts 8:36-39, I Corinthians 11:23-26).

Last Things

We believe in the personal and visible return of the Lord Jesus Christ to earth and the establishment of His kingdom. We believe in the resurrection of the body, the final judgment, the eternal joy of the righteous, and the endless suffering and separation of the lost (Acts 1:11, Isaiah 9:6-7, II Peter 3:7, John 3:16).

Christian Liberties

We believe in the personal Lordship of Christ over individual believers. Each believer must give account for himself to Christ. Therefore, in matters not strictly defined in Scripture, convictions of one should not be imposed on others (Romans 14).

ARTICLE I: MEMBERSHIP

Section 1: Membership and Requirements

Membership in the church family is open to those who meet the following requirements:

a) Profession of faith in Jesus Christ as Savior and Lord

b) Completion of membership class requirements as outlined in church ministry documents

A list of members who are actively participating in church ministries will be maintained.

Section 2: Dismissals

Membership may be terminated in the following ways:

a) Member initiates request for membership termination
b) The Elders may remove a person's name from membership after appropriate efforts to restore fellowship and participation have failed. There shall be no time limit, but shall be up to the discretion and good judgment of the Elders.
c) The Elders may dismiss a member as part of a disciplinary action.

ARTICLE II: GOVERNMENT

Section 1: The Headship of Christ

The government of CVCC will seek to maintain the Lordship and direction of Jesus Christ as the Head of this Body. Those in authority will continually seek His mind and His will, through His Spirit and His Word in all actions and decisions.

Section 2: The Board of Directors and Elders

The Board of Directors and Elders oversee and govern the ministry of the church by precept and example under the Lordship of Christ and through the leadership of the Pastor. They will pray together regularly and review the progress of the ministry. They will gather together for prayer and counsel on a regular basis, at least monthly.

Subject to the limitations of the Articles of Incorporation, other sections of the bylaws, and of Nevada law, all corporate powers of the corporation shall be exercised by or under the authority of, and the business and governance affairs of the corporation will be managed by the Board of Directors. Without limiting their general authority, the Board of Directors shall have the following authority:

a) To select and remove all other officers, agents and employees of the corporation; prescribe such powers and duties for them as may or may not be inconsistent with the law, the Articles of Incorporation or the Bylaws and fix their compensation.

b) To conduct, manage and control the activities and business of the corporation; and to make rules and policies not inconsistent with the law, Articles of Incorporation, or the Bylaws.

c) To borrow money and incur indebtedness for the purposes of the corporation, and for that purpose to authorize to be executed and delivered, in the corporate name, promissory notes, bonds, debentures, deeds of trust, mortgages, pledges, or other evidences of debt and securities.

The Board of Directors will consist of those persons nominated and elected by the Board members then serving. The Board of Directors will consist of at least two members.

To be selected as an Elder, a man must meet the qualifications outlined in Scripture in 1 Timothy 3:1-7 and Titus 1:5-9.

There will be a minimum of at least two and no more than fifteen Elders. Additional Elders may be added by the procedure described below. The Pastor and a majority vote of the Elders then serving will nominate elders. The voting members of the congregation present shall ratify election of Elders at a scheduled membership meeting.

Regular meetings of the Elders may be held at any place and at any time designated by the Elders in writing at least four days before the meeting. A quorum of the Elders will be a simple majority of those Elders then serving. The Pastor or any two (2) may call special meetings at any time other Elders.

An Elder, other than the Pastor, may be removed from office by the vote of a majority of the Elders then serving. The Pastor may only be removed by a two-thirds (2/3)-majority vote of the voting membership of the church present at a meeting called in accordance with Article 4. Elders will receive no compensation for their services, but may be reimbursed for expenses. Elders who also serve as officers may be compensated.

ARTICLE IV: OFFICERS OF THE CHURCH

Section 1: Officers

The officers of this corporation will be a President, Secretary and Treasurer. The Board of Directors may also appoint other officers as they may deem necessary. No person, other than the President, may hold more than one office.

Section 2: Election

The Pastor shall serve as the President of the Corporation. The Board of Directors shall elect by simple majority vote the Secretary, Treasury and any other desired officers of the corporation from their number at the first meeting of each year. The term of office is to be one year, or until their successors are elected and qualified.

Section 3: President (Pastor)

Subject to ratification of the Board of Directors, the President shall have general supervision, direction, and control of the business and activities of the corporation. He shall be responsible for the presidency of all meetings of the membership, Elders, and shall have other powers and duties as may be prescribed from time to time by the Elders.

The primary ministries of the pastor are to be the lead visionary, teacher, and equipper. He will give himself to the ministry of the Word and prayer. He will teach, guide, and lead the church to fulfill the vision for ministry that God has entrusted to him and to this Body. As president, he also serves as the Chief Executive Officer of the Board and Chair of the Elders. He is responsible to supervise and provide direction for any other staff and or ministries of the church.

71

In the event of a vacancy in the office of President (Pastor), the Elders shall develop a committee to search for a successor Pastor. Once the right candidate is found (either within the Body or from outside candidates), the candidate will be presented to the church membership. A 75% vote of those voting members present (with at least a quorum of 30% of the voting membership present) will be required to elect a new President.

The pastor is to be compensated by written agreement with the Board of Directors. Compensation, benefits, and expenses provided will include (as God supplies the resources): housing allowance, salary, health insurance, retirement, continuing education and other reasonable ministry expenses. The written agreement is to be reviewed no less than annually.

If a termination of the pastor is to be considered, it requires the call of at least two Elders to initiate a meeting of the Elders. The meeting shall be called in accordance with the procedure for establishing a special meeting. Should three-fourths (3/4) of the Elders concur that the pastor should terminate his pastoral leadership of the church, the matter will be brought before the voting membership at a duly called meeting. A two-thirds (2/3) majority of the voting membership (with a quorum of 30% of the voting membership present) will be required to terminate the pastoral ministry.

Section 5: Other Ministerial or Support Staff

The Pastor may present other ministerial or support staff to lead the ministry. Each staff person so presented will have duties and compensation reviewed by the Board of Directors prior to approval of the position. All staff members serve under the Pastor's direction and supervision, and at his pleasure.

Section 6: Vice President

In the absence or disability of the President, the Vice-President shall perform temporarily all the duties of the President, and in so acting shall have all the powers of the President until the Board of Directors take action on the vacancy. The Vice President may have such other powers and perform other duties as may be prescribed from time to time by the Board of Directors.

Section 7: Secretary

The Secretary shall keep a full and complete record of all the proceedings of the Board of Directors; shall keep the seal of the corporation and affix it to such papers as may be required in the regular course of business; shall make services of such notices as may be necessary or proper; shall supervise the keeping of records of the corporation; and may have other such duties as prescribed by the Board of Directors.

Section 8: Treasurer

The Treasurer shall receive and safely keep all funds of the corporation and deposit them in the bank or banks that may be designated by the Board of Directors. Financial procedures, as indicated in these bylaws or in policies adopted by the Board of Directors shall be followed in the disbursement of funds.

ARTICLE V: FINANCIAL SUPPORT AND FISCAL YEAR

This church shall operate on a calendar year from January 1st through December 31. This church shall be supported through the tithes and offerings of its members and friends.

ARTICLE VI: MISCELLANEOUS

Section 1: Execution of Documents

The Board of Directors may authorize by majority vote any officer or officers, agent or agents, to enter into any contract or execute any instrument in the name of, and on behalf of the church and such authority may be general or confined to specific instances. Unless so authorized, no officer, agent or other person shall have any power or authority to bind the church by any contract or engagement or to pledge its credit or to render it liable for any purpose or to any amount.

Section 2: Inspection of Bylaws

The church shall keep in its principal office the original or a copy of its Articles of Incorporation and Bylaws, as amended to date, certified by the Secretary, which shall be open to inspection by the members at all reasonable times during the office hours.

Section 3: Construction of Definitions

Unless the context otherwise requires, the general provisions, rules of construction and definitions contained in the Nevada Nonprofit Corporation Law shall govern the construction of these Bylaws.

Section 4: Rules of Order

The rules contained in Roberts Rules of Order, as most recently revised, shall be the general guide to govern all business and/or Board meetings of the church, except in instances of conflict between said Rules of Order and the Articles of Incorporation and Bylaws of the church or provisions of law.

Section 5: Dissolution & Non Profit Status

The property of this corporation is irrevocably dedicated to religious purposes and no part of the net income or assets of the organization shall ever inure to the benefit of any director, officer or member thereof or to the benefit of any private person.

The Board of Directors shall make a recommendation regarding dissolution to the membership; said action to be approved by a two-thirds (2/3) vote of the membership. On the dissolution or winding up of the corporation, its assets remaining after payment of, or provision for payment of, all debts and liabilities of this corporation, shall be distributed to a non profit fund, foundation, or corporation which is organized and operated exclusively for religious purposes and which has established its tax-exempt status under section 501(c) 3 of the Internal Revenue Code.

Section 6: Liability

No officer, Director, Elder, or representative appointed by this church shall be personally or individually liable for any error, mistake, act of omission for, or on behalf of this church, occurring in the scope of his or her duty as such officer, Director, Elder, or representative, excepting only for his or her own willful misconduct or violation of law.

ARTICLE VII: AMENDMENT OF BYLAWS

These bylaws may be amended or repealed and new Bylaws adopted by the Board of Directors provided said amendments or new bylaws shall have been presented in writing to the Board. Adoption of amendments or new bylaws shall require a three-fourths (3/4) vote of the Board of Directors.
Amended: 11/96, 6/97, 11/99

DR. JOHN JACKSON

Receipt Procedure for First Contributions

Carson Valley Christian Center Receipting & Office Procedures: 11/97

Contributions/Financial Transaction

1) Enter person's data into Membership Plus(Parsons Software Program) if not already done

2) Enter pledge and or contribution into Membership Plus(or other software package)...contribution to household

3) Enter information into thank you letter, print, and mail
Acknowledge all out of town gifts, any first time gifts, and any gifts over $200(IRS requirement)
Give Pastor a list of all people who gave $100 or more

4) Prepare Bank deposit and copy all checks and deposit slip

5) Enter Deposit into Quickbooks (accounting package), properly allocating sources

CVC Vision: Update 8/99

Carson Valley Christian Center will bring people to relationship with Jesus Christ through relational and event evangelism

Disciples will grow through systematic teaching and application of Biblical principles to daily living

Since the first days of the emerging ministry vision at CVC, we have built on two cornerstones: 1) Passionate evangelism focus through relationships and special events and, 2) High impact teaching and application of the Bible to daily life.

The ministry that has emerged at CVC during these past 18 months has exceeded even our grandest dreams. We have dared to dream of what God might do, and He has exceeded even those dreams. At the 18-month mark of our public launching, we find ourselves in the midst of a tremendously fruitful harvest. This has been exhilarating to be sure, and it has strained our leadership infra structure at many levels.

We are now at a critical turning point. In the next 3-6 months we will likely move into our new facilities and may see growth that exceeds even the pace of these previous months. Determining how we effectively reach and minister to those God is entrusting to us is of the greatest importance to those of us in leadership. The times call for decisive leadership.

Listed below are the broad outlines of where I sense we should go from a program and emphasis standpoint. I would like concerted prayer to take place over these next 7 days on these matters. We will take our staff time on the 24th to cover these matters.

Program Direction:

-Massive focus Fall 99 on Sunday morning. Two services with "Can't Miss" experienced during the first half of the services and dynamic teaching each week. Increased use of video and drama. Children's ministry broken down in smaller age groups with a redoubled commitment to excellence. We must meet our quality benchmarks in each class.

-Focus on Discipleship Fall 99. Identify 50 people who can take others through 1-1 or 1-3 Basic Discipleship. Move people from Basic Discipleship to 9 week course in groups of 3-5. Following groups of 3-5 completing Discipleship course, have them commit to being Disciplers

-Minimal commitment to Small Groups in Fall of 99. Maintain 3-5 existing groups with 1-2 additional ones available on Wednesday for the Fall.

-LIFT Rallies held once monthly in Fall: September 5th at the Property: Focus on Prayer and Fasting for Evangelism, October 3rd focus on Worship, November 7th focus on Ministry, December 5th focus on Community.

-Major Prayer Movement developed Fall 99. Develop Sunday morning prayer teams

-Launch "Whole Lotta Life" campaign Fall 99

-Staffing Priorities: Identify key players from outside. Identify future roles of Roy, Jack, Lex, Keith and have deployed by mid 2000.

-Launch Midweek Believers Service in 2nd week of January, 2000. Focus will be on extended worship with prayer opportunities ("come forward to pray with prayer counselors, healing of heart, mind, and body"), and teaching that will be deep and hard hitting. We will see about NOT providing childcare, but providing an overflow room for parent's with children and allowing parents to sit with children in the auditorium as well.

-Focus on reducing debt from Fall 99 to Fall 2001. Goal in 2 years? Pay off $1.6 million in debt in order to prepare for capital campaign late 2001.

CVC Goals

Because God has seen fit to exceed what was apparently our smallish understanding of His vision for this ministry, we have revised our goals as follows:

Original Goal: * Reach 1000 Adults in weekend worship within 5 years of our first public worship service

Revised Goal: * Reach 5000 people in weekend worship services by the 5th birthday of our public launch (February, 2003)

Original Goal: * Have a minimum of 20 acres of property, with worship center seating capacity of 1000

Revised Goal: * 40 acre campus with worship center seating capacity of 2000 by 7th birthday

Original Goal: * 40% of those attending worship be previously Unchurched

Original Goal: * 50% of those attending weekend worship using spiritual gifts for ministry, involved in a small group, and have completed personal discipleship training

Original Goal: * Plant one new church per year after five years

Revised Goal: *Partner in planting 5 new churches per year via leadership, finances, or internships

CVC Values

1) Evangelism occurs primarily in relational contexts in family, work, neighborhood, and community settings and secondarily in outreach events that are easily accessible to seekers

2) God's Word is consistently and relevantly taught in corporate worship, small groups, classes, personal discipleship, and through creative activities.

3) Performing Arts are honored and utilized to the glory of God in a fashion relevant and accessible to seekers

4) Community life in the church family is so honored that division and gossip are confronted quickly, clearly, and resolved in accordance with Biblical principles of fellowship and conflict resolution

5) Spiritual gifts discovery and utilization are essential aspects of discipleship for every believer

6) Ministry programs and activities are started, led, and grown by gifted men and women from the church family

7) Support ministries are led by people with serving gifts. These people are regularly honored and affirmed

8) Pastoral staff model ministry values of team, affirmation, and excellence through their teaching and relating with the church family

9) We honor those God has gifted and called to authority. Those in authority exercise their leadership with humility and grace as servant-leaders

10) Stewardship of God's financial resources is practiced, modeled, and taught with passion and clarity

5 G's for Health at Carson Valley Christian Center (CVC, Adapted from WillowCreek Community Church)

Our vision for ministry states clearly that we want to see non-Christian people become disciples of Jesus Christ. But it is sometimes difficult to describe just what a disciple "looks like". Listed below are five characteristics that we are aiming to have present in our family here at CVC:

Grace-We believe that everyone is lost and separated from God. Only by God's wonderful and grace filled gift of Jesus Christ are we able to be in right relationship to Him. Only by His continuous gifts of grace are we able to be forgiven and to live in grace filled relationships with other people.

Growth-We believe that every Christian should develop spiritual habits that draw them into closer fellowship with Jesus. These habits include Bible Study, Prayer, Fellowship, and Stewardship.

Groups: We believe every disciple should engage in meaningful relationships with other Christians where authentic love, accountable relationships, and Godly counsel are present

Gifts: We believe that God has uniquely gifted and shaped every Christian. Spiritual gifts are entrusted to believers for effective service of Christ in the world and in the church. Discovery and use of spiritual gifts is an essential dimension in the life of a disciple.

Giving: We believe that an essential part of the adventure in knowing God is learning to trust Him with finances. Tithing (giving 10%) of one's income through the church and giving more when the Spirit prompts is a special dimension of spiritual health and joy intended for every believer.

DR. JOHN JACKSON

People Pathway at Carson Valley Christian Center
Reaching Carson Country for Christ (8/99)

1) Believers enter into a Relationship with Unchurched Friends

2) Believers share a verbal witness with Unchurched Friends

3) Believers invite Unchurched friends to a special event or weekend service

4) Unbelievers accept Christ as Savior

5) New Believers enter into Basic and Extended Discipleship relationships

6) Believers understand the cycle of reproduction and move to #7 and #1

7) New Believers attend Midweek Services
Believers develop healthy spiritual habits

8) Believers discover gifts and fulfill their kingdom purpose

Principles for Launching a Ministry at CVC (updated 5/99)

While God grants vision to an individual, He brings confirmation through others. Translation: If God is birthing a ministry in our midst, we want to see a "team" approach to ministry leadership. The key ministry leader should have completed all the Discovery Classes through Discovery 301.

We believe God wants things done "decently and in order". Therefore, we take pains (!) to insure that ministries are well planned, well publicized, and well conducted. It is often helpful to start small and then move forward from there ("crawl before you walk, walk before you run").

Every ministry at CVC is ultimately related to a staff pastor or elder. A new ministry needs to be coordinated with a staff pastor, not for "control" sake, but for coordination sake. A staff pastor can assist with #1 & #2 above, but WILL NOT "run" the new ministry. We expect and believe in God raising people within the body to lead ministries

Any ministry developed and conducted by CVC must be led by leaders who are in agreement with the CVC vision for ministry and in appropriate submission to the leadership of the church family.

Every ministry at CVC needs to have a "pastoral care" component. In other words, when people participate in a ministry, we want them to have regular contact, opportunity to pray with others, and a vehicle with which to communicate to the elders and staff pastors.

Financial needs and program support should be shared with a staff pastor, who then will bear responsibility to "carry the ball" of the financial need through the church administrative structure. Appeals for financial support to the general church membership will not be made and other types of appeals (to more limited groups) must be cleared by the staff pastor.

Characteristics of Involvement Levels at CVC

1. Core
Attend regularly
Have completed 301
Desire to serve in ministry
Prepared to commit 10 hours a week to ministry (includes weekend services)
Understand the commission and vision of CVC, and own it.
Ability to lead, teach, disciple, pray, help, serve
Staff, pastors, congregational leaders and support persons.
Help lead and coordinate small group and topical activities.
Members of the church
Should have a deeper personal prayer and study life than most. A model for others.
Look at life as a ministry. Wholistic view of ministry that incorporates their entire life.
Live as a witness for Jesus daily in all walks of life.
Are at a place in their walk with God that reproach is not placed upon His name by their lifestyle.
Have committed their lives to Jesus, and are sold out to Him.
Have accepted the responsibility and call to serve God in their lives.
Continually renewing their commitments to give God complete control of their lives.

2. Committed

Regularly attend weekly weekend services
Completed 101 and 201
Good percentage attend small group studies, topical group studies
(single, marriage, etc.)
or other growth opportunities. They experience "community."
Help with event evangelism efforts. Give extra effort to "arrive early and
stay late."
Members of the church in most cases.
Have a developing personal prayer and study life.
Working on living for Jesus daily
Moving toward a lifestyle that does not bring reproach upon the name of
Christ.
Have committed their lives to Jesus.
Attend lift most of the time.
Living for God is becoming more important in their lives
Sense a responsibility to live for the Lord and move in a direction to
serve Him.
Working on giving God complete control of their lives.
Understand the vision of CVC, and where we are headed.

3. Congregation

Attend fairly regularly
Have attended 101
Have committed their lives to Jesus.
Are members of the church
Occasionally attend other studies and opportunities for growth.
May attend LIFT from time to time.
Lifestyle may be questionable, and may cause reproach upon His name in some cases.
May not have a very active prayer or study life.
Have a "Sunday is enough" mentality
Many are not members of the church.
Have not been convicted of the call to give all of their lives to Christ and His control.
May not understand the vision of CVC.
Some level of false doctrine, wrong thinking present.

4. Crowd

Less committed than the congregation
Attend periodically, and they are fine with that.
Probably most do not know Jesus as their savior.
Not church members
Do not normally attend other studies and growth opportunities.
Not sure where they stand with God.
"Seeking something....is it God?" mentality
Not willing to yield much to God yet.
Unbelief, false doctrine, wrong thinking prevalent.
Life styles across the board.
"Weekends once in a while" mentality.
Testing the water when they attend.
Includes some Christians looking for a home church.
Have not attended any of the 01 classes.
Spiritual "things" are only a part of their multi-faceted lives.

5. Community

The harvest field!
Do not attend CVC
Some have heard about CVC but have not attended yet.
May come to some of the annual events but don't attend a service or study.
Some have family and friends that attend in all four of the above categories.
Mostly Unchurched.
Not convinced Jesus is who He said He was.
Confused by pluralism vs. genuineness.
View "church" as a sub-culture. Universalist approach to salvation.

"2nd Anniversary Dream Teaching"

At our second birthday, I had the opportunity to remind our people and community of God's work and the importance of having a dream. As you read this excerpt of my teaching for that day, begin to consider what dreams God is birthing in you:

"Today we want to welcome you to our field of dreams. We want you to know that we built this for you, and you are welcome here! God is a God of dreams! He places them in the heart of people and gives them the power to see them accomplished. God wants you to dream His dreams! Just over 20 months ago, we established this church, launching it into public view on February 22, 1998. Today, we stand at this significant moment celebrating all that we have experienced together. Here, in our Grand Opening, we want to pause and remember some significant things about where we have come from and what we have learned."

"DREAM"

Devote yourself to God's game plan

For I know the plans I have for you," declares the LORD, "plans to prosper you and not to harm you, plans to give you hope and a future. Then you will call upon me and come and pray to me, and I will listen to you. You will seek me and find me when you seek me with all your heart." (Jeremiah 29:11-12)

God has plans for us that are full of a future and a hope. God so desperately wants us to know the joy and peace that come when we are driving down the "centerline" of our lives.

<u>Respond</u> to God's signals!

"I thank my God every time I remember you. In all my prayers for all of you, I always pray with joy because of your partnership in the gospel from the first day until now, being confident of this, that he who began a good work in you will carry it on to completion in Christ Jesus"(Philippians 1:6)

We have had two key thoughts since our first days together: 1) Determine not to get in God's way(for instance, we don't let our shoe tell our feet how big to be; likewise we don't want to tell God how large this church can be…it can be as large as He wants it to be!), and 2) Find where God is at work and go there! Celebrate and join in His working.

<u>Eagerly</u> celebrate the wins in life!

"'For this is what the Sovereign LORD says: I myself will search for my sheep and look after them. As a shepherd looks after his scattered flock when he is with them, so will I look after my sheep. I will rescue them from all the places where they were scattered on a day of clouds and darkness. I will bring them out from the nations and gather them from the countries, and I will bring them into their own land. (Ezekiel 34:11-13a)

"I tell you that in the same way there will be more rejoicing in heaven over one sinner who repents than over ninety-nine righteous persons who do not need to repent."(Luke 15:7)

We have understood that the greatest thing that we can experience is the power of a changed life. Many in our midst have literally had their lives changed by God's power. NOTHING is more important in our midst than a person who does not know Christ coming to know Him. That is worth a party!

How many of you have made a commitment to know Christ or have decided to renew and return to your relationship with Christ since coming to CVC? (people all over the auditorium raised their hands at this moment...it was powerful!)

Activate your faith!

"We live by faith, not by sight" (II Corinthians 5:7)

"I have fought the good fight, I have finished the race, I have kept the faith." (II Timothy 4:7)

Charles Swindoll met a person who was on the board of Walt Disney's early years. Occasionally Walt would come to the board with an idea that was so "out there" Board members would literally shift in their seats, and look, glassy eyed in response. Even considering such a thing was beyond their wildest imaginations. The Board member recalled that unless every person raised strenuous objections, Walt Disney would not pursue the idea.

Mobilize your life around Knowing Him!

"Not that I have already obtained all this, or have already been made perfect, but I press on to take hold of that for which Christ Jesus took hold of me. Brothers, I do not consider myself yet to have taken hold of it. But one thing I do: Forgetting what is behind and straining toward what is ahead, I press on toward the goal to win the prize for which God has called me heavenward in Christ Jesus." (Philippians 3:12-14)

This is our single greatest reason for being. We are not building an institution, an organization, a club, or a cartel. We are building an army of people who desperately want to see people have their business lives changed, who want to see their families have hope, and who want to have their relationships with others be on solid ground. The key to all of this is in being rightly related to God. Until you know peace, you will ultimately have no peace.

Launch Team Roles
Carson Valley Christian Center
1997/98

First Touch Ministry:
-Coordinator
-Parking Lot Greeters
-Information Table Staff
-Refreshment Table Staff
-Guest Attendants

Gift Mix: Exhortation, Helps

Discovery 101 Team:
-Facilitator
-Class Hosts
-Follow-up Teams

Gift Mix: Helps, Pastoring, Evangelism

Discovery 201 Team
-Facilitator
-Class Hosts
-Group Facilitators

Gift Mix: Pastoring, Knowledge, Teaching

Nursery Ministry:
-Coordinator
-Helpers

Gift Mix: Helps, Mercy

Discovery 301 Team:
-Facilitator
-Ministry Placement Counselors

Gift Mix: Teaching, Helps, Administration

Children's Ministry
-Coordinator
-Ages 2-3
-Ages 4-5
Gift Mix: Teaching, Mercy, Helps

Youth Ministry:
-Parent Helpers
-Youth Workers

Gift Mix: Teaching, Helps, Administration

Music & Worship Ministry
-Worship Team & Band
-Sound Techs
-Video Techs
-Set-up & Tear Down Teams

Gift Mix: Exhortation, Helps, Discernment

Support Team:
-Clerical Support
-Custodial Support

Gift Mix: Helps, Exhortation, Giving

DR. JOHN JACKSON